HUMAN RESOURCES

in leisure and tourism

JOHN EDMONDS

Hodder & Stoughton
A MEMBER OF THE HODDER HEADLINE GROUP

Acknowledgements

The author and publishers would like to thank the following for permission to use material in this book:

Justin Fleming, Nick Munday, David West and David Anderson at Panorama Holiday Group Ltd for Figures 1.5, 1.6, 1.7, 2.2, 2.3, 3.2, 3.3 and 3.4; Horsham District Council for Figure 1.2; Guildford Spectrum Leisure Centre Complex for Figures 1.3 and 2.1; Pearson PLC for Figure 1.4; Hodder & Stoughton Educational for Figure 3.1; the Sports Council for Figures 4.1 and 4.4; the *Independent on Sunday* for Figure 3.5; the *Observer* for Figure 5.1; Butlins for the illustration entitled 'The road ahead' on page vi; the Life File Photo Library for Figure 1.1 and the image of a British Airways aeroplane on page vi.

British Library Cataloguing in Publication Data
Edmonds, John
  Human resources in leisure and tourism. – (Hodder GNVQ.
  Leisure & tourism in action)
  1.Tourist trade – Employees 2.Tourist trade – Personnel
  management
  I.Title
  338.4'791'0683

ISBN 0 340 65836 3

First published 1996
Impression number   10 9 8 7 6 5 4 3 2 1
Year   1999 1998 1997 1996

Copyright © 1996 John Edmonds

All rights reserved. No part of this publication may be reproduced or transmitted in any form or by any means, electronic or mechanical, including photocopy, recording, or any information storage and retrieval system, without permission in writing from the publisher or under licence from the Copyright Licensing Agency Limited. Further details of such licences (for reprographic reproduction) may be obtained from the Copyright Licensing Agency Limited, of 90 Tottenham Court Road, London W1P 9HE.

Typeset by Wearset, Boldon, Tyne and Wear.
Printed in Great Britain for Hodder & Stoughton Educational, a division of Hodder Headline Plc, 338 Euston Road, London NW1 3BH by Bath Press.

Contents

Assessment matrix i
Introduction: the human factor iv

1 *People and pyramids – organisational structures* 1
   Why organise? 1
   Case study: Panorama Holiday Group – a company profile 7

2 *Teams – greater than the sum of the parts* 14
   Why teams? 14
   Case study: The Panorama Telephone Sales Team 15

3 *Square pegs into square holes – recruitment and selection* 24
   Choosing the best person for the job 24
   Case Study: Panorama Holiday Group: recruiting and selecting overseas representatives 25

4 *Rules and regulations – workplace standards and conditions* 43
   Joining the organisation 43

5 *Review of the Unit* 53

Useful addresses 56
Glossary 57
Index 58

Assessment Matrix

The tasks contained in this book will generate the evidence indicators of each element of Unit 2: *Human Resources in the leisure and tourism industries*, part of the Advanced GNVQ (Applied A Level) in Leisure and Tourism (1995 specifications). They also meet performance criteria of the Key Skills elements indicated (the term *Key Skills* is used instead of *Core Skills* throughout – element numbers refer to 1995 specifications).

Students may provide evidence to meet grading themes through each task. Tasks 1, 5 and 6 involve complex activities and are most likely to generate evidence at Distinction level.

Key Skills Hint boxes precede certain tasks to give help and guidance on the particular skill developed through the task.

Task	Unit 2	Key Skills		
		Application of Number	Communication	Information Technology
Task 1	2.1			
Task 2	2.2			
Task 3		3.2 pcs 1–9		
Task 4	2.3		3.1 pcs 1–5 3.2 pcs 1–5	
Task 5	2.4			3.1 pcs 1–5 3.2 pcs 1, 2, 4–7 3.3 pcs 1–6
Task 6	Review of Unit			

Introduction: The Human Factor

The workforce of a leisure and tourism organisation are its **human resources.** They are the most important and costly ingredient within the product offered to the customer.

Leisure and tourism are industries dedicated to customer enjoyment. Whether front-of-house or backroom, staff provide the human factor which can make or break the customer's leisure experience. The workforce is a valuable and expensive asset to an organisation – employees' wages may account for more than 75 per cent of running costs. However, unlike physical resources such as buildings and equipment, which become obsolete in time, human resources can grow in value through experience and training.

Human resource management, or **HRM**, is concerned with all aspects of staffing an organisation. In many businesses HRM has replaced the term *personnel management*. The change in terminology has reflected a move away from the traditional role of hiring and firing of staff. Instead, HRM takes a wide-ranging view of the complex needs of both employee and organisation to encompass staff recruitment, retention, motivation, discipline, reward, training and development. Organisations acknowledge business success depends heavily upon giving staff the conditions to perform to their full potential. This in turn has placed greater emphasis on the skills of managing people well.

Conducting your own research

A case study of Panorama Holiday Group Ltd is used throughout the book to illustrate human resource issues and provide a real-life scenario for the tasks you will undertake. Panorama Holiday Group is a tour operator offering package holidays to a variety of winter and summer destinations. It is a **private sector** organisation within the *travel and*

VI

THE HUMAN FACTOR

The world's favourite airline? Not before it put people first. Faced in the early 1980s with falling market share and poor customer relations, British Airways introduced company-wide 'Putting People First' and 'Managing People First' training programmes. Seminars focused on quality of customer service, staff teamwork and effective management. The retrained workforce has helped turn the airline into a successful company in the 1990s.

tourism industry.

Several tasks will ask you to contrast the Panorama case study with a **public sector** *leisure and recreation* organisation of your choice. You might select a local authority leisure services department, leisure centre, museum or arts centre for example. Your research would benefit from a visit to the organisation and/or a presentation by a *representative* at your school or college.

You will need to research the following topics (more details are given in the tasks):

- how the organisation is structured (Task 1)
- ways in which teams of staff operate (Task 2)
- how the workforce is recruited and selected (Task 4)

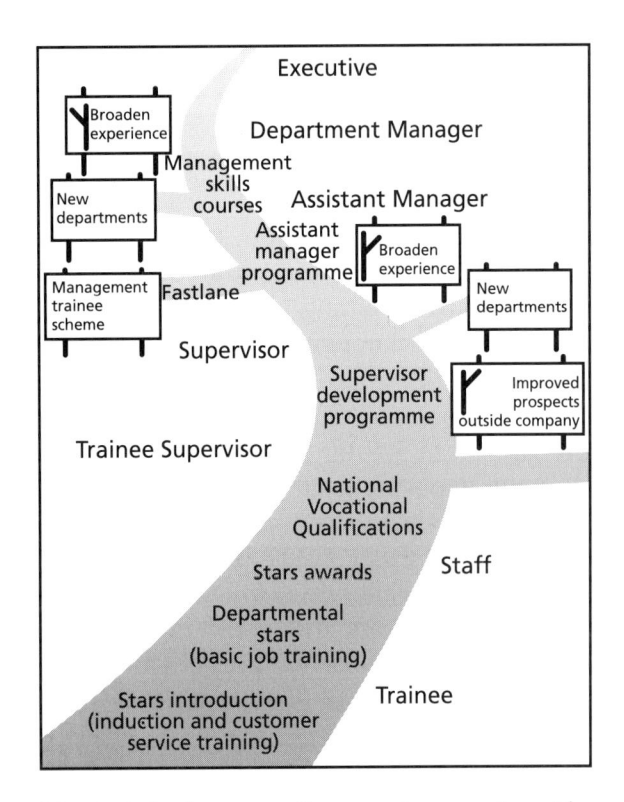

The road ahead: career pathways and progression with experience and training at Butlin's Holiday Worlds

SECTION 1

People and Pyramids – Organisational Structures

Key Aims

This section will help you to:

- identify types of organisational structures found in the leisure and tourism industries
- explain influences upon, and impacts of, different organisational structures
- identify key job roles within private and public sector leisure and tourism organisations
- research and compare the structures of two leisure and tourism organisations

WHY ORGANISE?

Organisations are made up of a number of individuals working together to achieve a common purpose. They are ever-present in our daily lives, both in and out of the workplace, and vary greatly in size and complexity. Using the definition above, clubs, schools, colleges, even families can all be viewed as organisations. Indeed, simple non-industrial examples may help us make sense of complicated business structures.

The rugby scrum in Figure 1.1 may seem a disorganised mass of heaving bodies to the non-player. But in fact each pack of forwards displays a tight **organisational structure** which should:

- provide a means of achieving the group's aim, in this case winning the ball!
- define the relationships between different parts of the organisation – how the forwards mesh and bind together within the scrum and how they link with the rest of the team

HUMAN RESOURCES IN LEISURE AND TOURISM

FIGURE 1.1 *A number of individuals working together to achieve a common purpose!*

- establish clear lines of communication – so that, at a given signal, the pack will drive forward together as the ball is fed into the scrum
- clarify positions of decision-making, authority and responsibility within the team
- establish patterns of control within the organisation – this may extend outside the team to include the coach or manager
- identify each individual's role and positional duties.

The same justifications apply to the organisational structure of a leisure and tourism enterprise. It provides the framework within which staff work together. As for the rugby team, the success the organisation enjoys will depend greatly upon effective communication and clear appreciation of roles and responsibilities.

Organisational charts

The clearest way of illustrating an organisation's structure is by an organisational chart. It indicates sub-divisions and levels of responsibility within the workforce. However, two points should be borne in mind when using charts:

1. a chart illustrates the structure at a given time. Organisations are constantly evolving to meet both internal and external changes, and so each chart should be viewed as a current snapshot which may alter in time

2. charts indicate the formal structure of an organisation. Staff will also develop a network of informal relationships within the workplace that cannot easily be represented diagrammatically, but which may be as influential in decision-making and communication.

Types of organisational structures

Organisations exhibit one or more of a variety of structures. Figures 1.2, 1.3 and 1.4 illustrate the different structures of three leisure and tourism organisations.

Horsham Museum

Type(s) of structure
Horsham Museum has a simple *flat* structure with few levels of responsibility (see Figure 1.2 opposite). The Curator is the principal source of authority within the immediate organisation, although he or she will report to the Leisure Services Manager and Director of Leisure Services, both officers of the local District Council.

This structure is highly *centralised* in that responsibility and decision-making are largely centred upon the Curator.

Factors influencing structure
The small number of personnel and size of

PEOPLE AND PYRAMIDS – ORGANISATIONAL STRUCTURES

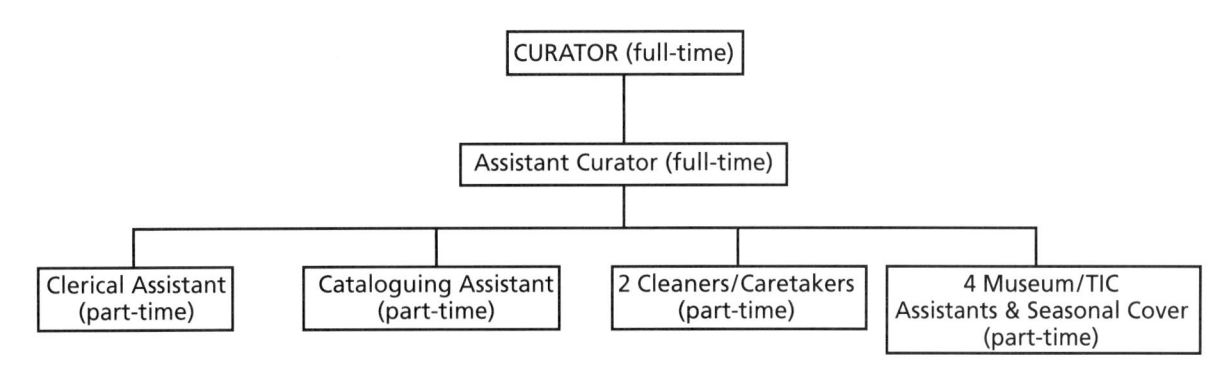

```
                    CURATOR (full-time)
                            |
                  Assistant Curator (full-time)
                            |
    ┌───────────────┬───────────────┬───────────────┐
Clerical Assistant  Cataloguing    2 Cleaners/      4 Museum/TIC
  (part-time)       Assistant      Caretakers       Assistants & Seasonal Cover
                    (part-time)    (part-time)      (part-time)
```

FIGURE 1.2 *The organisational structure of Horsham Museum*

the organisation does not necessitate a complex staffing structure. The staff shown in Figure 1.2 are augmented however, by as many as 45 volunteers who work in the museum on a weekly or fortnightly basis, and who are managed by the Curator, Assistant Curator and Cataloguing Assistant.

Impacts of structure

The small number and close proximity of staff promotes a flexible, communicative, team approach to the running of the museum. Each understands the others' roles and is able to stand in for absent colleagues. The Curator enjoys much autonomy in managing the museum, but lacks the feedback and support of a number of assistant managers that would be characteristic of a bigger organisation.

Guildford Spectrum Leisure Centre

Type(s) of structure

Guildford Spectrum Leisure Complex has the tall structure of a larger organisation (see Figure 1.3 on page 4). Staff are sorted into several layers of responsibility, each answering to the level above. The number of personnel decreases at each higher level, creating a pyramid or *hierarchical* structure. This structure is also centralised in that major decision-making is concentrated at the highest levels.

Figure 1.3 is also a *functional* structure. Apart from horizontal levels according to responsibility, the workforce has also been divided vertically into departments, each with a specialist function: marketing, sports operations and so on.

Factors influencing structure

The multiplicity of management levels is explained by the concept of **span of control**. This is the number of subordinate staff supervised by any manager. Should this number become too great, the manager will not be able to monitor the work of all the staff, and efficiency will suffer as a result. One solution is to create an additional layer of assistant managers or **supervisors** who will monitor a smaller span of control, and who in turn are supervised by the manager.

Impacts of structure

A hierarchical structure may provide ready-made replacements from a lower level as staff changes occur. However, the transfer of information within the organisation can become ineffective as communications are sifted through a number of managerial layers – think of the game Chinese Whispers! New ideas and innovations may be stifled if they cannot easily be communicated to major decision-makers.

Pearson plc

Type(s) of structure

Organisations that become too tall risk becoming bureaucratic. Figure 1.4 illustrates a popular response – a flattened, *decentralised* and *divisional* structure which creates independent units under the control of a parent holding organisation.

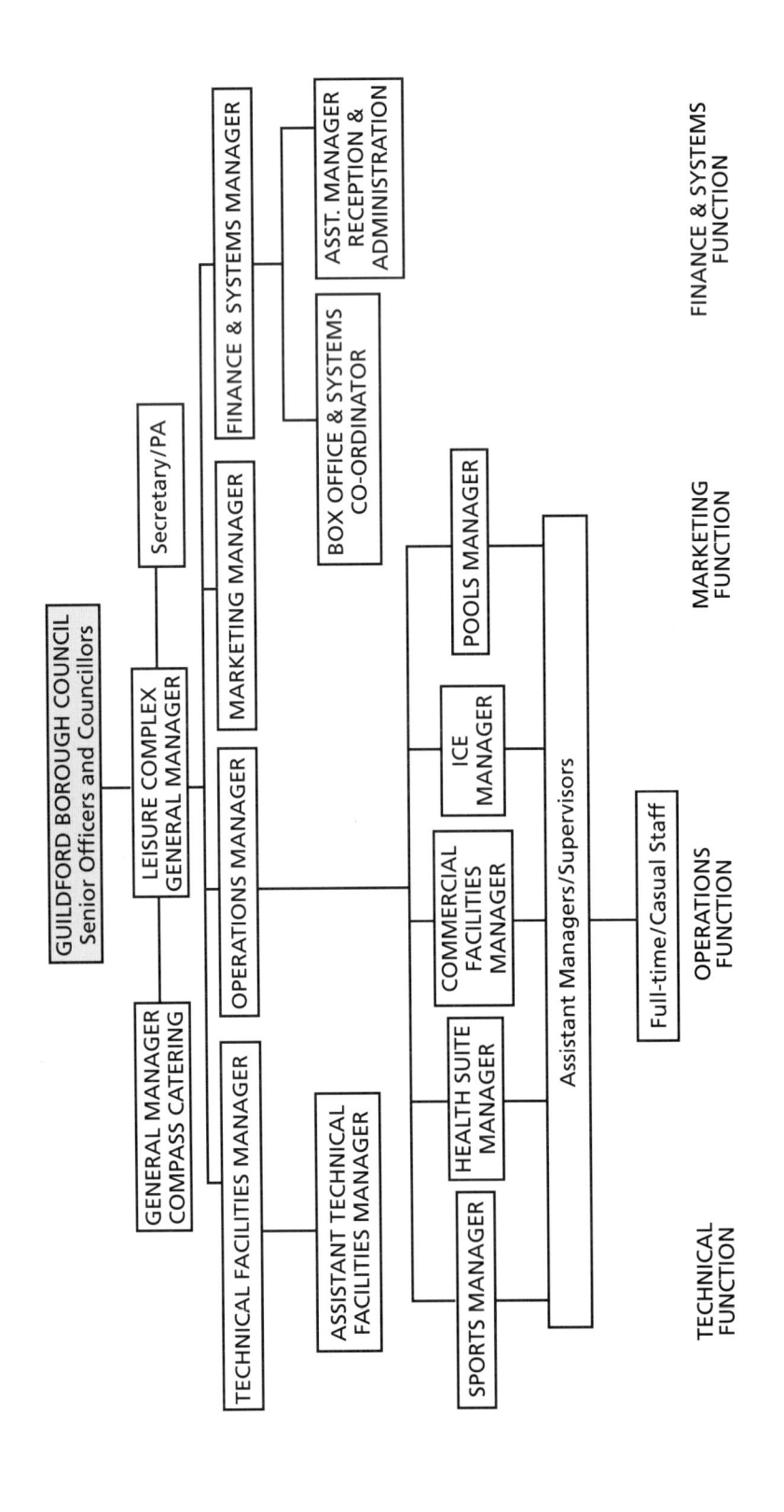

FIGURE 1.3 *The organisational structure of Guildford Spectrum Leisure Complex*

PEOPLE AND PYRAMIDS – ORGANISATIONAL STRUCTURES

Factors influencing structure

Divisions can be created on the basis of function, product, service or location. They may be formed due to changes in ownership, for example, as one organisation acquires another company which it then operates as a subsidiary. Each attraction in Figure 1.4 has a separate product and location and is run as an individual operation.

Impacts of structure

Decentralised structures may be more economical as they reduce the number of management levels required. They serve to motivate divisional managers who have greater freedom to make their own decisions. They allow increased specialisation towards specific markets.

Factors influencing organisational structures

The examples above illustrate a variety of internal (inside the organisation) and external (outside the organisation) factors which can influence the structure of a leisure and tourism enterprise. For example, the size of the organisation has an immediate bearing on the complexity of the structure required. A list of potential factors includes:

- the size of the organisation
- its location
- the products or services it offers
- the management style(s) used
- the ownership and sector of the organisation
- competition from rival enterprises
- changes in market trends, population patterns, new technology, a change in government or new EU or government directives.

Certain factors in this list are straightforward to identify within a given organisation. Others are more complex to analyse and require a degree of tact on the part of the observer! The management style of senior personnel can have a significant influence on organisational structure and the approach taken to HRM. Researchers have identified different management styles within organisations:

- *authoritarian*: the leader or manager takes all decisions and issues instructions to staff without consultation
- *consultative*: the leader consults with other staff but remains the sole decision-maker

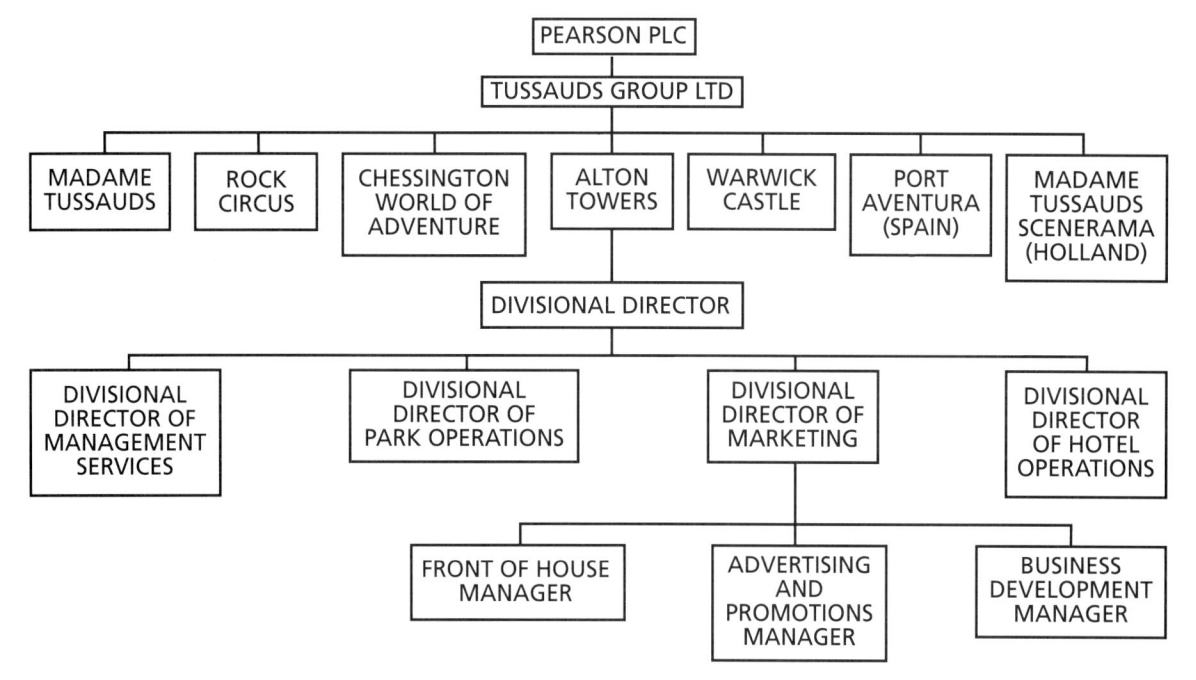

FIGURE 1.4 *The leisure and tourism interests of Pearson PLC*

- *democratic*: the leader involves staff in discussion and decision-making and implements the group decision
- *passive/laissez-faire*: the leader chooses to intervene in the work of other staff as little as possible

We can expect authoritarian and consultative styles commonly to result in centralised organisational structures, whereas more decentralised patterns will emerge if democratic or passive styles are employed.

Impacts of organisational structures

Figures 1.2, 1.3 and 1.4 also give an indication of how different types of structure impact on the way an organisation operates. For example, communication between staff can be a simple or complex operation depending upon organisational structure. A list of internal and external impacts can be drawn up:

- on work relations
- on job opportunities
- on communication
- on decision-making
- on how the organisation responds to internal changes in staff or management
- on productivity and profitability
- on how the organisation responds to external changes in markets, government, technology or competition.

The impact of the organisational structure on work relations may be difficult to assess when researching a leisure and tourism facility. Two types of formal work relationships can be identified. The first is the vertical *line relationship* between each member of staff and the *line manager* they are directly accountable to. This illustrates the *Scalar principle*, a management theory which states that efficient organisations result from clear, unbroken chains of authority within the workforce.

Other work relationships link departments horizontally and are called *staff relationships*. For example, human resource staff may operate on behalf of other departments in an organisation by recruiting, selecting and training employees. You might find it interesting to research if there is a link between either line or staff relationships and organisations with centralised or decentralised structures.

Key job roles within leisure and tourism organisations

All public companies are required by the 1985 Companies Act to form a board of at least two **directors** (private companies may have only one director). The role of the board is to determine the policy of the company and protect the interests of the **shareholders** (owners). One member of the board is elected Chair to lead board meetings and act as the company's front person. The **Managing Director** has overall responsibility for the operation and performance of the business. Full-time directors actively engaged in running the company are termed **executive directors**. Those who attend board meetings on a part-time basis are **non-executive directors**.

The management and resourcing of leisure and tourism provision in the public sector is undertaken through different roles and processes. Decision-making at local authority level is undertaken by **councillors** within leisure committees. Putting the decisions made into practice is delegated to a Director of Leisure Services (or similar job title) and other senior personnel such as Tourism Officers and Leisure Centre General Managers (see Figure 1.3). **Compulsory Competitive Tendering (CCT)** has allowed private firms to provide local authority services, blurring the boundaries between the private and public sectors.

The role of **managers** is recognised across sectors. Managers are responsible for the day-to-day decisions and running of a department or function within an organisation. Key managerial duties include:

- implementing the policies and instructions of the Managing Director or General Manager
- ensuring the department functions effectively and reaches agreed targets
- motivating staff and communicating the organisation's policies to them
- allocating work between staff, and being involved in their appointment, promotion and dismissal.

PANORAMA HOLIDAY GROUP – A COMPANY PROFILE

The case study of Panorama Holiday Group is featured in all four Sections of this book. Figure 1.5, an extract taken from the company's staff handbook, gives a detailed introduction to the company. Figure 1.6 illustrates the company's organisational structure and Figure 1.7 shows the distribution of its operations at the time of writing.

Panorama employs a workforce in the Brighton office of more than 70, a further 15 staff in the Dublin office and over 70 resort-based managers and representatives.

The two executive directors are its principal shareholders. One director, Justin Fleming, takes the combined roles of Chair and Managing Director. As the directors own the major share of the company, decision-making tends to be heavily focused at the top management levels.

Staff are grouped vertically in departments. Department managers are directly accountable to one or both of the two executive directors. Managers are assisted by one or more supervisors, depending on the span of control in each department. The structure of the company has evolved rapidly. Expansion has required new specialist staff to be appointed and departments to be created. The newly-formed Personnel and Training department, for instance, now takes on some of the HRM issues, such as recruitment and selection, formerly handled by other departments. A technology manager has been recently appointed to develop the full potential of the company's in-house computer network and to utilise the 'information super-highway' of the Internet.

Department managers meet weekly as a team with the directors, and individually with a director each month. The weekly meetings foster communication between departments and directors, and across departments. The monthly meetings allow manager and director to appraise the performance of the department. Mid-term departmental targets are reviewed and set on a six monthly basis.

Resort-based staff are managed by the Overseas department based in Brighton. There is regular communication between head office and the resorts by fax, telephone and company mail (using the charter flights leased by the company), and through manager visits. Resort staff however, are able to operate more independently due to distance from the UK.

PANORAMA

MISSION STATEMENT

To give exceptional personal service in providing good value travel arrangements to our customers without whom there would be no reason for our Company to exist.

In achieving the above objective it is our aim to generate a level of profit which enables the Company to grow, maintain its financial independence, and improve the prosperity of the shareholders, employees and those associated with the business.

PANORAMA - A BRIEF HISTORY

Many years ago, Adrian Hayes was ordered to visit a warm and sunny climate in order to convalesce. He travelled from his family home in Hove, East Sussex, to a tiny fishing village in Northern Spain. This little village, Lloret de Mar, housed just one small hotel and a few fishermen's cottages dotted along the wide sweep of a sandy bay.

Adrian Hayes was so taken with Lloret that he bought a small villa for future visits. He talked about his idyllic retreat on the, as yet undiscovered, Costa Brava so often that many of his friends asked if they could rent the villa for their own holidays. Adrian agreed. He organised rail transport for the continuously growing number of visitors to Lloret and by 1954, had set up one of the earliest Tour Operations in the UK, Panorama Holidays.

Due to Adrian's charisma and popularity plus the hard work of all the Hayes family, Panorama grew rapidly to include many other Mediterranean destinations and the Company soon became one of the top ten UK Tour Operators.

In 1976, Justin Fleming joined Panorama. He worked hard and was soon promoted to the position of General Manager. Nick Munday joined in 1981 as Management Accountant, later to become the Company's Financial Controller and Company Secretary.

Justin Fleming had always wanted to run his own company. In 1986 he left Panorama and bought the controlling interest in Young World Holidays from its founder, John Lucraft. Nick joined Justin in 1987 as Commercial Director and bought a minority share in Young World from him. By 1988, Young World Holidays had progressed to such an extent that it was able to purchase the Tour Operating Division of Panorama Holidays and in 1988 changed its name to the *Panorama Holiday Group Ltd*.

The ski programme is the only product to have survived from the early days of Young World Holidays which was dedicated, as the name suggests, to the youth market. Recognisable brand names from those early days include Camp Africa, Greek Village and Suncamps. During the 1980s, as the youth market contracted, Young World Holidays, now under the direction of Justin Fleming, began to cater for family holidaymakers and the Tunisia Experience programme was set up. This was quickly followed by other 'Experience' brands including, Ibiza, Ceylon, and Golf. Panorama's renamed Ski Experience operation continued to expand as the specialist to Andorra. The operation includes successful programmes to both Livigno and Sauze d'Oulx in Italy.

FIGURE 1.5 *Extract from the Panorama staff handbook*

Panorama - A Brief History (page 2)

In 1995, a corporate rebranding exercise resulted in the 'Experience' title being dropped giving more emphasis to the Company name and specific destinations or products. For the 1996/97 season, the Panorama brochure has been renamed as Panorama Ski and Snowboard in recognition of 'boarding' as a growing sport. Killington in Vermont, the largest ski area on America's Eastern Seaboard has been added.

Today, the Panorama Holiday Group is still independent. The owners are Justin Fleming, John Lucraft and Nick Munday. The original owners, the Hayes family, live in Ibiza where they act as Panorama's agents - they own much of the property featured in the Panorama Ibiza programme. Adrian and Audrey Hayes still take great pleasure in welcoming clients to Ibiza, many of whom have been travelling with Panorama for more than twenty-five years.

Those associated with the Panorama Holiday Group can not only look back with pride over the last forty years or so but can also look forward to an exciting future with one of the top twenty operators in the UK. In 1995 Panorama carried more passengers than ever with a turnover in excess of £25 million.

Panorama is the top independent operator to Tunisia and prides itself on being the specialist to this exotic year-round destination. The Panorama Golf programme takes advantage of the abundance of Tunisian courses and ideal wintersun climate. The Ibiza programme continues to grow, due, in no small part, to the unique link with the Hayes family and, with the addition of Majorca and Menorca, a well balanced portfolio is offered in the Balearics. The ski programme, has become exceptionally popular due to both excellent skiing conditions in recent years and the good value of duty free resorts. As well as departing from 6 mainland UK airports, Panorama has grown from strength to strength in Ireland with flights from Dublin, Cork, Shannon and more recently, Belfast.

In 1991 Panorama, with the aid of a local GSA, opened a tiny office in central Dublin to sell Tunisian holidays departing from Ireland. Bookings exceeded all expectations and in just three years the now restructured Irish operation very successfully expanded to include the ski and Balearic islands products as well as Tunisia.

One of Justin's first projects when he moved to Young World Holidays in 1986 was to open a Travel Agency called Brighton Travel Shop. In 1992 the Company also bought the original Panorama Travel Agency in Hove and renamed it Hove Travel Shop. These two travel agencies are thriving concerns and give the Company Directors a valuable insight into, and firsthand knowledge of, the retail trade.

The Panorama Holiday Group is a member of the Association of British Travel Agents (ABTA), the Federation of Tour Operators (FTO), The Association of Independent Tour Operators (AITO), the International Air Transport Association (IATA), and holds a licence granted by the Civil Aviation Authority (CAA). The Brighton and Hove Travel Shops are members of the Alliance of Independent Travel Agents (ARTAC). Panorama's Directors have always taken a keen interest in trade affairs: Justin Fleming has served on the AITO Council and is entrenched in ABTA affairs where has held National Council office. He was Chairman of the Tour Operators Council at ABTA for many years. He is also Vice-chairman of FTO.

HUMAN RESOURCES IN LEISURE AND TOURISM

Justin Fleming — Chairman and Managing Director

- **Martin Young** — Marketing Manager
  - DTP
- **Shirley Briggs** — Customer Service Manager
- **David West** — UK and Overseas Personnel and Training Manager
- **Paul Riches** — National Sales Manager
  - **Peter Kirk** — Groups Manager
  - **Jackie Winter** — Telephone Sales Supervisor
  - **Mark Hopper** — Agency Sales Support Manager
- **Susan Guarracino** — Customer Relations Manager

Nick Munday — Director

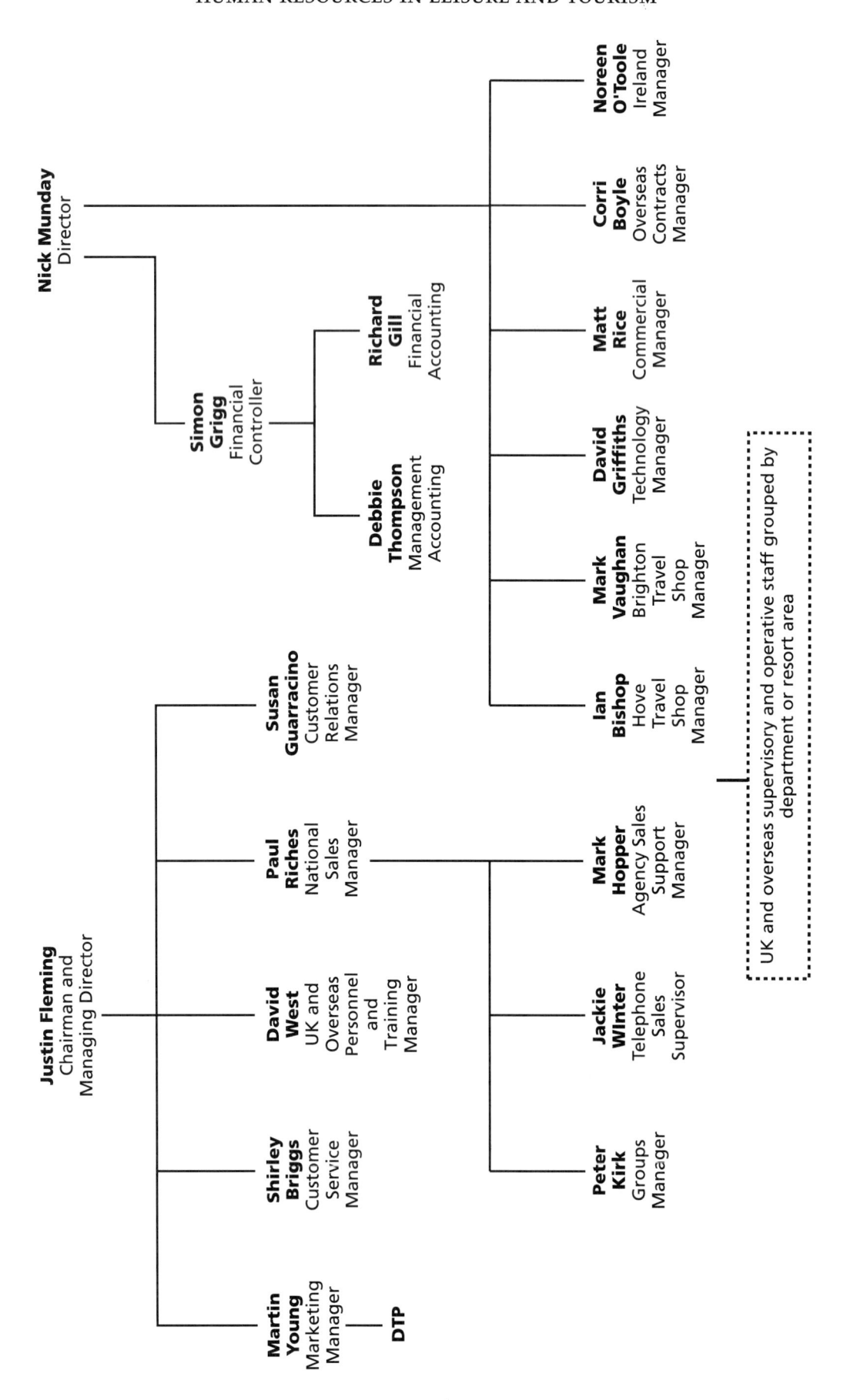

- **Simon Grigg** — Financial Controller
  - **Debbie Thompson** — Management Accounting
  - **Richard Gill** — Financial Accounting
- **Ian Bishop** — Hove Travel Shop Manager
- **Mark Vaughan** — Brighton Travel Shop Manager
- **David Griffiths** — Technology Manager
- **Matt Rice** — Commercial Manager
- **Corri Boyle** — Overseas Contracts Manager
- **Noreen O'Toole** — Ireland Manager

UK and overseas supervisory and operative staff grouped by department or resort area

FIGURE 1.6 *Organisational structure of Panorama Holiday Group*

PEOPLE AND PYRAMIDS – ORGANISATIONAL STRUCTURES

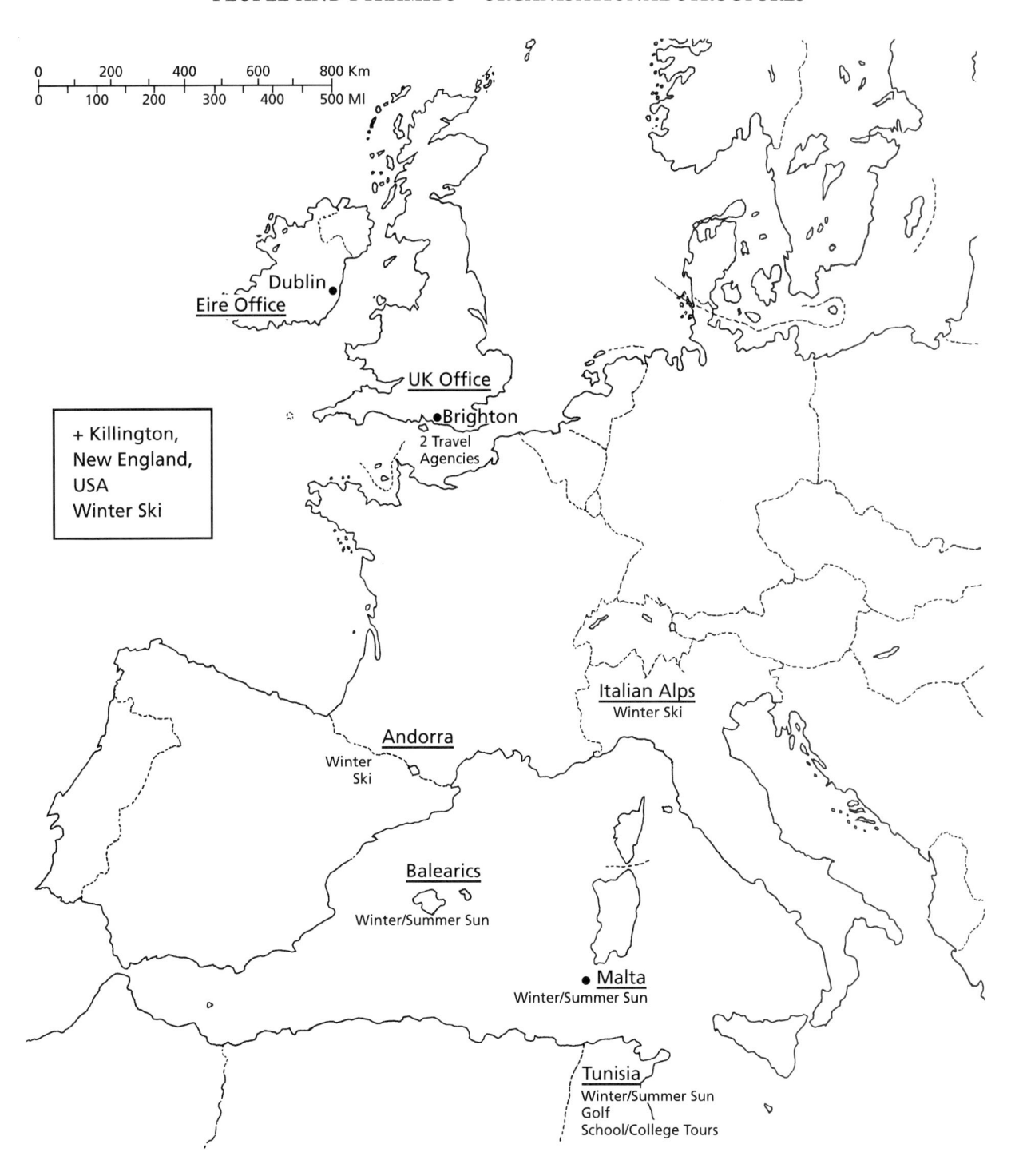

FIGURE 1.7 *Panorama Holiday Group operations*

HUMAN RESOURCES IN LEISURE AND TOURISM

TASK 1

A TIME TO RESTRUCTURE?

For this task you are asked to take the role of a management consultant. You receive the following memo from Panorama Holiday Group:

MEMO

TO: Peoplepower Management Consultants Ltd
FROM: Panorama Holiday Group Ltd
REF: Organisational Structures Survey

We have been reviewing the present organisational structure of the company for some time, but we feel we need some more information before we can decide on any changes. This is where you come in!

We would like you to address these points:

1 What are our options?
- Briefly describe the possible types of organisational structure available to us (even those you think inappropriate)
- Describe the factors that could influence our choice of each structure
- How could each structure impact on the way the company operates?

2 Comparisons
- Research the structure of a public sector leisure and recreation organisation and compare it to Panorama. I enclose a draft copy of an analysis sheet to aid your research (Figure 1.8). Devise your own version to identify the principal factors that have (i) influenced the structure and (ii) the impacts the structure has on the operation of the facility. Complete your sheet using questionnaire or interview responses of staff working in the organisation
- Complete a second copy of your analysis sheet for Panorama based on the information provided (pages 7–11)
- How do we compare? In what ways are we different? How are we similar? Include organisational charts in your report to illustrate your comparisons
- Who are the equivalents, within the leisure and recreation organisation, to our directors, managers, and supervisors? How do their roles and responsibilities compare?

3 Recommendations
- What brief recommendations would you make based on your research? Should we stay as we are? Is there scope for an alternative structure? How could your research have been improved?

Your findings should be compiled into a word processed report which I can circulate to fellow directors and managers within the company. The report should be concise and to the point – we haven't time to read lengthy documents!

CHECKLIST OF PORTFOLIO EVIDENCE

- ☑ Word processed report including organisational charts and analysis sheets.
- ☑ Action plan and research notes.

PEOPLE AND PYRAMIDS – ORGANISATIONAL STRUCTURES

ORGANISATIONAL STRUCTURE ANALYSIS

Organisation:
Sector:

Type(s) of organisational structure:

How significant is each factor in influencing the structure of the organisation?
(tick one box for each category)

	weak ▷ strong	Explanatory comments
size	☐☐☐☐	
location	☐☐☐☐	
nature of product	☐☐☐☐	
nature of service	☐☐☐☐	
management style	☐☐☐☐	
ownership	☐☐☐☐	
competition	☐☐☐☐	
change	☐☐☐☐	

To what extent does the structure of the organisation impact upon…?
(tick one box for each category)

	weak ▷ strong	Explanatory comments
work relations	☐☐☐☐	
job opportunities	☐☐☐☐	
communication	☐☐☐☐	
decision-making	☐☐☐☐	
response to internal changes	☐☐☐☐	
productivity	☐☐☐☐	
profitability	☐☐☐☐	
response to external changes	☐☐☐☐	

FIGURE 1.8 *Organisational structure analysis sheet*

SECTION 2

Teams – Greater than the Sum of the Parts

Key Aims

This section will help you to:

- understand the structure and purpose of different leisure and tourism teams
- identify the relationships between roles, responsibilities and team objectives within facilities
- identify lines of authority within teams and organisations
- describe factors which promote or hinder the effectiveness of teams
- use mathematical techniques to devise an incentives scheme for a staff team

WHY TEAMS?

Leisure and tourism personnel commonly operate in teams within the overall structure of their organisation. Teamwork is essential if a facility is to function successfully. Think of the close co-operation within an aircraft cabin crew to ensure passengers travel safely and comfortably. Such teamwork does not happen by chance, but is the result of intensive training and a mutual appreciation of the need to work together.

Leisure and tourism students can develop their teamwork skills through organising and running an event. This section may help you, therefore, in preparing or evaluating your efforts towards the *Event management* unit.

Working as a team offers a variety of

benefits to both organisations and team members:

- improved efficiency – collective efforts usually complete tasks more quickly and effectively than when undertaken by several individual workers – making the team 'greater than the sum of the parts'
- potential for creativity and innovation – ideas for improving practices can come from any team member and be communicated more easily – for example, the use of quality circles in which staff brainstorm ideas for improvement in work practices
- covering for absent staff – team members can act as substitutes for others in the team as necessary
- job satisfaction – on the whole, people enjoy working with colleagues on a social level
- shared responsibility – a sense of belonging to a team can motivate staff to make extra efforts and raise the quality of service offered to customers

Two types of teams can be identified in leisure and tourism. **Organised teams** are set up to work on continuous or long-term projects, often within a departmental framework. An example is the Panorama telephone sales team featured in this section.

Other teams may be established for a set period to complete short-term projects or plan special events. These are called **ad hoc** or **project teams**. *Ad hoc* is Latin for 'to or for the purpose'. Such teams are the product of a further type of organisational structure shown in Figure 2.1 – the **matrix structure**.

The matrix structure draws on specialist staff from different departments or divisions within an organisation. Together, they are able to respond quickly to market changes or increased competition, develop a product or plan an event. In the example shown in Figure 2.1 the successful organisation of the basketball match involves the combined efforts of a project team from a variety of departments.

Productive teamwork is a skill requiring insight and understanding to fully develop.

The following case study provides an in-depth investigation of one staff team.

THE PANORAMA TELEPHONE SALES TEAM

Booking a holiday

Visit a local travel agent to watch customers buy a package holiday. Almost invariably the travel consultant will refer to a VDU to check the availability of flight seats and accommodation, and then complete the booking by keying in the client's details. The VDU is connected via a modem to the computer reservation systems (CRS) of major airlines and tour operators. Bookings made by travel agents are automatically logged into an operator's mainframe computer and the information is used to issue tickets and invoices.

Clients may have particular queries or requirements not met by the information to hand on the travel consultant's viewdata screen. In this case, the consultant will contact the tour operator's reservations department for further details.

The telephone sales team at Panorama's Brighton office sits at a series of open plan desks equipped with telephones, keyboards and viewdata screens. The Panorama operator can communicate with the travel consultant by telephone and on the consultant's viewdata screen. Queries can be answered, special requests recorded and the booking confirmed by the telephone sales operator.

The telephone sales team handle general enquiries for information or brochures from the public or travel agents. Approximately 10 per cent of clients book flights or holidays direct by post or telephone. Operators are responsible for *product delivery* and *customer care*. They must have specialist knowledge of the company's products and be able to tailor these to client's needs. Like all of Panorama's workforce, telephone sales staff are encouraged to take two educational trips to resorts each year to update their knowledge at first hand.

The telephone sales room can be a noisy, bustling environment. There is a constant influx of calls on the eight telephone lines

HUMAN RESOURCES IN LEISURE AND TOURISM

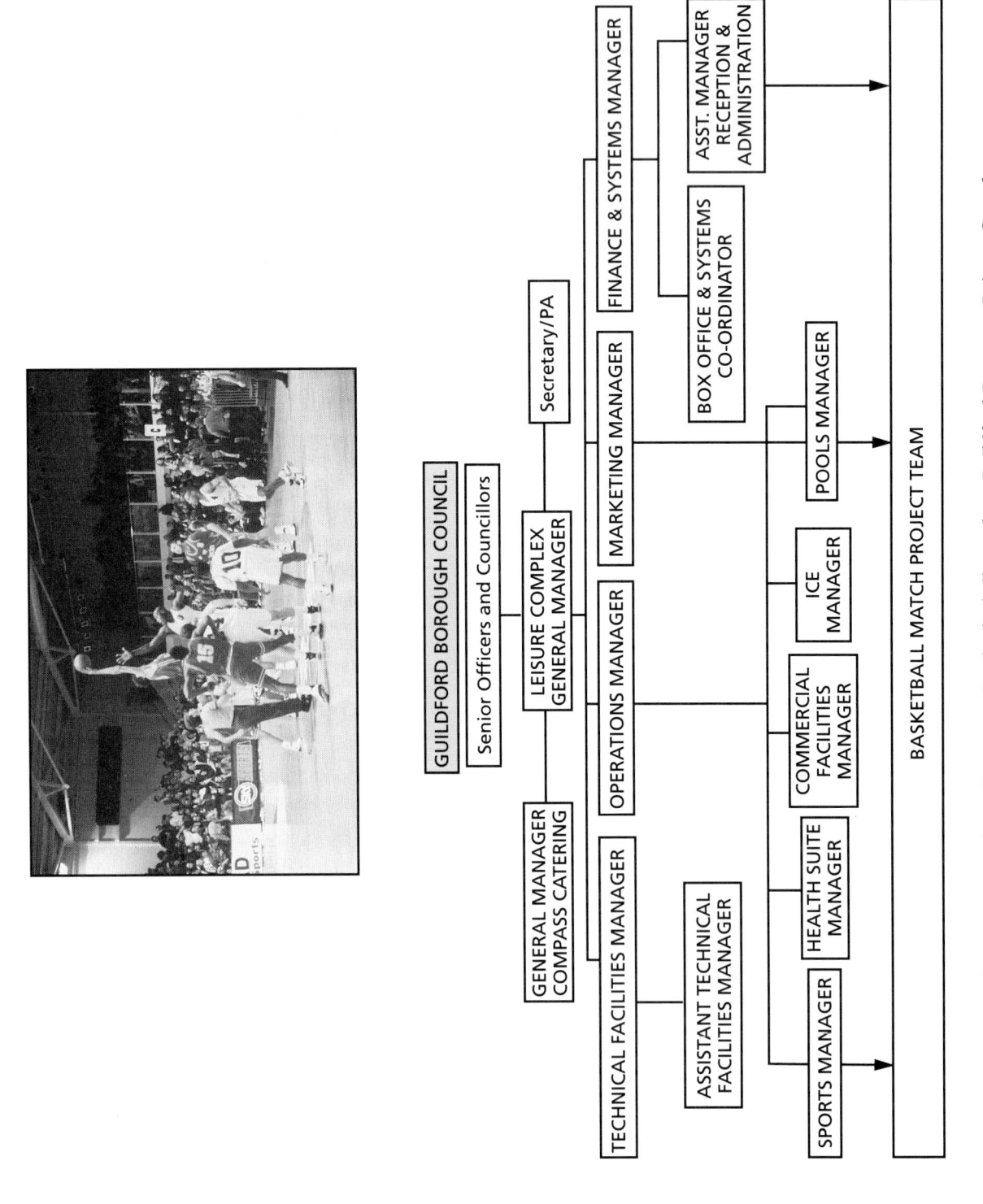

FIGURE 2.1 *A matrix organisational structure: staging a European Cup basketball match at Guildford Spectrum Leisure Complex*

TEAMS – GREATER THAN THE SUM OF THE PARTS

FIGURE 2.2 *Members of Panorama's reservations team at work*

during busy periods. A call sequencing system is used to automatically route an incoming call to a free operator. The team's supervisor is able to monitor calls through a switchboard and ensure all telephones are answered as quickly as possible.

Roles and responsibilities

Figure 2.3 indicates clear **lines of authority** within the team linking managerial, supervisory and **operative** levels. These in turn form part of the line relationships within the company as a whole (see Figure 1.6). The telephone sales supervisor is accountable to the national sales manager for the performance of her team. An incentives scheme is used to encourage the team to meet performance targets set by the manager (see Task 3).

The telephone sales supervisor has a key role in the team's functioning. There are seven full-time operators, augmented by four part-time and two Saturday staff. The supervisor devises a staff rota for set tasks and to cover lunch times, evening duties and days off. She produces a team handbook and in conjunction with the personnel and training manager trains new operators to use the CRS. She undertakes regular staff appraisals to evaluate and encourage the work of individual operators. She communicates both upwards and downwards within the team, meeting weekly with the manager to report on team performance, and relaying company policy and directives to the operators.

Both manager and supervisor must be prepared to demonstrate control within the team, whilst striving for a positive working atmosphere. The supervisor must 'crack the whip' if phone calls remain unanswered. The

```
                            Directors
                               ↑
                    ┌──────────────────┐
                    │ National Sales   │
                    │    Manager       │
                    └──────────────────┘
                               │
┌──────────────┐    ┌──────────────────┐    ┌──────────────┐
│ Personnel and│----│ Telephone Sales  │----│  Technology  │
│Training Mgr. │    │    Supervisor    │    │   Manager    │
└──────────────┘    └──────────────────┘    └──────────────┘
                               │
```

full- full- full- full- full- full- full- part- part- part- part- Saturday Saturday
time time time time time time time time time time time

| Telephone Sales Operators |

—— line relationships
- - - staff relationships

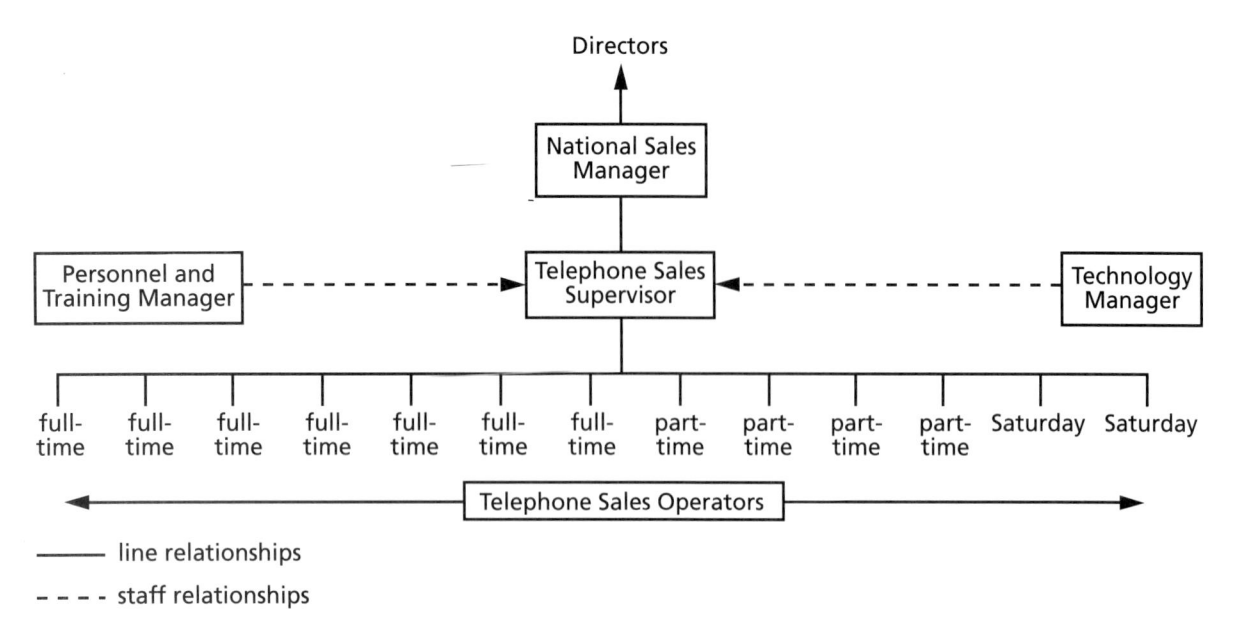

FIGURE 2.3 *Structure of the Panorama telephone sales team*

manager will deal with serious matters such as poor timekeeping or attendance. Both organise occasional evening social events to promote a team spirit amongst the operators.

Other staff have roles and responsibilities that support the team. The technology manager has a technical role in maintaining and developing the CRS. He provides a service to the *internal customers* – the other company staff. Access to data is restricted through personal passwords and menus customised for the telephone sales team. This promotes security of information and helps monitor the individual performance of each operator. Two departmental managers have company-wide health and safety responsibilities. They have ensured, for example, that the operators' viewdata monitors are fitted with screen filters. One telephone sales operator is an appointed first aider within the team.

Making an effective team

Several key factors can be identified that promote or hinder the effectiveness of the Panorama telephone sales team:

- *the working environment*: the telephone sales room is small and crowded for the number of staff present. Operators must talk on the telephone to clients in close proximity to each other, which can prove noisy and distracting. Communication and discussion within the team is highly effective however, which helps create a tightly-knit cohesive group
- *resources*: at present the operators lack headsets which would reduce distraction from ringing telephones and other staff. These are to be supplied and will allow calls to be routed through the headsets without sounding
- *processes*: the team have found the memory capacity of their present computers insufficient to store all CRS backup data. Instead they must use a time-consuming manual filing system to keep necessary information
- *team structure*: the incentives scheme helps motivate the team to support each other. Operators may be asked to undertake routine tasks in other departments during slack periods however, which can dilute the feeling of team spirit.

- *group dynamics*: working closely together can highlight individual differences and may lead to conflict. Teams are often most cohesive when members are of a similar age and/or background. The part-time operators tend to be older than the full-time staff and this can cause some division within the team. Staff appraisals, social events and joint educational trips help cement a team approach
- *management styles*: the open, consultative style used by the manager and supervisor relates closely to the team's needs and performance. On occasions this approach may be at odds with decisions made at a higher level by directors.

TASK 2

LEISURE AND TOURISM TEAMS IN ACTION

Your task is to present either a written or an oral report that investigates how leisure and tourism teams operate.

1 Types of teams

Provide a brief general description of types of teams including:

- their purposes and objectives
- factors that can influence their effectiveness

2 Team performance

Use the case study of the Panorama telephone sales team, plus an example of a staff team at your chosen leisure and recreation facility to:

- examine the roles and responsibilities of team members
- illustrate how these relate to the successful performance of the team
- identify lines of authority relating to each team using charts and explain the purposes of such structures – for control, for accountability, for communication, for responsibility or for monitoring and reporting

3 Team dynamics

The researcher Belbin (1981) suggested an effective team would include the following personality types, each contributing a different role within the team. He gave each a name to characterise their role:

- *the chairperson* – the team leader and co-ordinator
- *the shaper* – the task leader
- *the plant* – the ideas person
- *the monitor* – the person who checks the team's work
- *the company worker* – the organiser
- *the resource investigator* – the fix it person
- *the team worker* – resolves conflicts within the team
- *the finisher* – keeps the team on schedule

Give examples to identify any of these roles within a team you have studied or been part of – either in leisure and tourism or in your school or college.

CHECKLIST OF PORTFOLIO EVIDENCE

- ☑ Written report (approximately 1,000 words) or presentation notes and record of observation – either to include charts and illustrations.
- ☑ Action plan and research notes.

Key Skills Hint: Application of Number

Using the interquartile range and dispersion diagrams.

Analysing and comparing sets of data can be made easier if the *interquartile range* is calculated. This is the range between the *lower quartile* – the figure which appears one quarter of the way through the *ranked* data set – and the *upper quartile* – the figure which appears three quarters of the way through. The *median* and the *upper* and *lower quartiles* focus upon the middle 50 per cent of a data set and eliminate extreme high or low numbers that may distort overall trends. To calculate the interquartile range, the upper and lower quartiles must first be found. This is shown in the following example of a data set of 11 *ranked* values:

32
19
18 — upper quartile
16
14
13 — median (middle quartile)
10
9
7 — lower quartile
6
2

The upper quartile (UQ) is found using the formula:

$$UQ = \frac{(n+1)}{4}$$

where n is the number of values in the data set.

In the example above, $n = 11$, so

$$UQ = \frac{(11+1)}{4} = 3$$

This means the upper quartile is the third ranked number from the top of the data set, in this case 18.

The lower quartile (LQ) is found using the formula:

$$LQ = \frac{(n+1)}{4} \times 3$$

where n is the number of values in the data set.

In the example above, $n = 11$, so

$$LQ = \frac{(11+1)}{4} \times 3 = 9$$

This means the lower quartile is the ninth ranked number from the top of the data set, in this case 7.

The median, or middle quartile, is the mid point in the data set.

The interquartile range is the difference between the upper and lower quartile values, in this case: $18 - 7 = 11$.

The smaller the interquartile range, the more the values within the data set cluster close to the median.

Figure 2.4 illustrates a *dispersion diagram*, a useful way of plotting the interquartile range and median value graphically. The interquartile range is boxed and shaded for each data set – the resulting pattern is sometimes called box and whiskers. The diagram allows you to compare how the central values are grouped for a range of data sets – in comparing monthly figures for example, or between different categories, as in Figure 2.4.

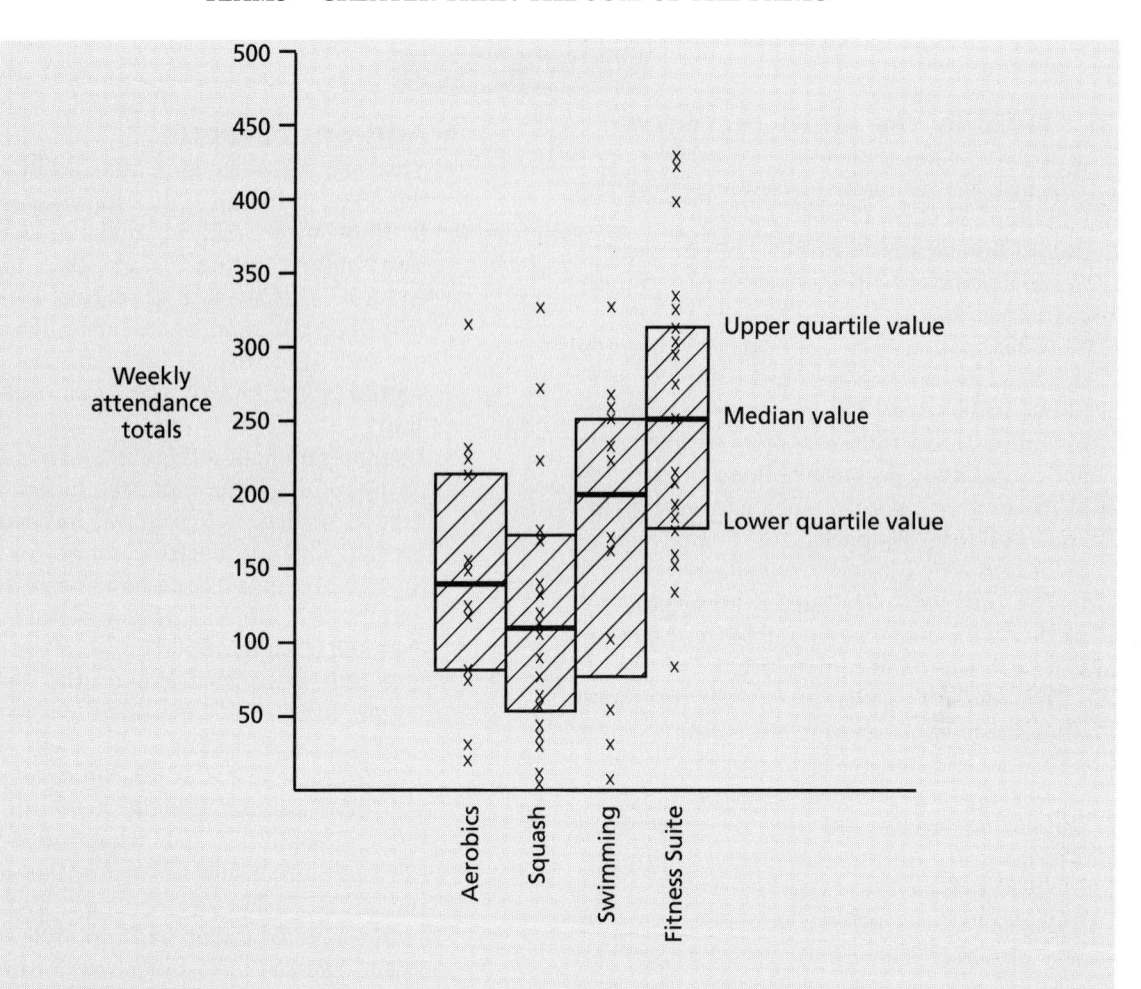

FIGURE 2.4 *Dispersion diagram to show leisure centre attendance patterns by activity*

HUMAN RESOURCES IN LEISURE AND TOURISM

TASK 3

FINDING THE RIGHT INCENTIVE

This task is a simulation based loosely on the Panorama Holiday Group case study. It illustrates how a team of staff can be encouraged to the benefit of both the company and individual employees.

As sales manager you wish to upgrade the existing incentives scheme for the telephone sales team. You are keen to increase revenue earned from *add-ons* – supplements above the basic package holiday price made at the time of booking, such as travel insurance, car hire, ski packs, full board supplements etc.

The directors have agreed a budget total of £6,000 for incentive payments to the reservations team in the coming year.

There are 13 operators in the telephone sales team in all. Seven are full-time, four part-time and two are Saturday staff.

Your task is to devise a new incentives scheme that will achieve the above aim. You should write a memo to the telephone sales team, clearly setting out the formula you propose.

Include the calculations you make to ensure your proposals fit within the agreed budget. Use checking procedures to confirm the accuracy of your working. Be aware of any accumulating errors that may result in your calculations should you use approximate figures or round up to the nearest whole number.

	Full-time Operator						
Month	1	2	3	4	5	6	7
January	82	50	78	73	95	76	99
February	81	54	46	56	77	86	97
March	51	49	43	48	62	78	72
April	40	26	30	33	43	57	48
May	37	32	24	30	45	43	59
June	43	41	51	31	35	47	61
July	46	39	47	49	44	51	58
August	52	52	50	53	45	61	68
September	54	49	58	61	59	73	66
October	47	31	43	38	44	64	59
November	41	34	29	41	43	48	49
December	30	33	24	39	41	46	50

FIGURE 2.5 *Revenue achieved by full-time operators by month in previous year*
NB: *all figures in £'000s*

1 Add-ons revenue

- You are keen to give an incentive to the team in the form of a monthly bonus if they meet add-on revenue targets. You must decide what the targets should be each month, bearing in mind that (i) certain months are busier than others and (ii) part-time and Saturday staff should be set lower targets than full-time staff

- Use the numbers in Figure 2.6 as a guide to the coming year. Plot each month's figures as a dispersal diagram. Indicate the median and interquartile range for each month. The graph axes have been drawn and the first month's figures plotted as an example in Figure 2.6(a).

- Use your graph to decide on the revenue targets for all full-time operators in each month of the coming year. Each target should be within the interquartile range for that month. Decide how big the bonus should be and what number of operators are likely to earn it. For example, if you decide on a £30 monthly bonus and set your target each month at the lower quartile, six staff should earn the bonus:

  6 × £30 = £180 per month × 12 = £2,160 per year

- Indicate your chosen monthly targets for full-time operators on a copy of Figure 2.6(b). Calculate similar targets for part-time and Saturday staff as ratios of the full-time targets:

  for part-time staff 1:0.85
  for Saturday staff 1:0.35

- Use the same bonus payment and expected success rate for part-time/Saturday staff as you chose for full-time staff. Calculate the expected monthly and annual total payments for part-time/Saturday staff and combine these with your full-time total

2 Setting out your proposals

- Ensure your bonus payments for add-ons targets do not exceed the £6,000

TEAMS – GREATER THAN THE SUM OF THE PARTS

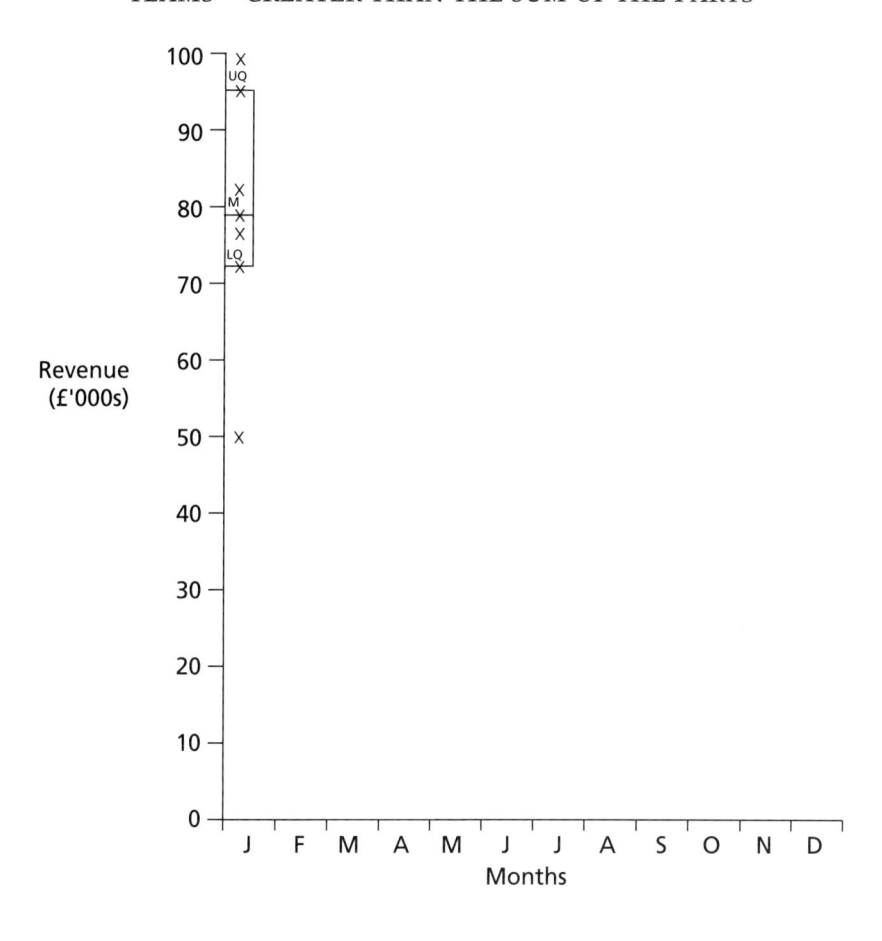

Revenue (£'000s) plotted against Months (J F M A M J J A S O N D). In January, data points are shown with UQ ≈ 95, M ≈ 80, LQ ≈ 72, and additional X markers around 78–98. A separate X is plotted at approximately 50 in February.

(a) Dispersion diagram of revenue earnings by full-time operators by month

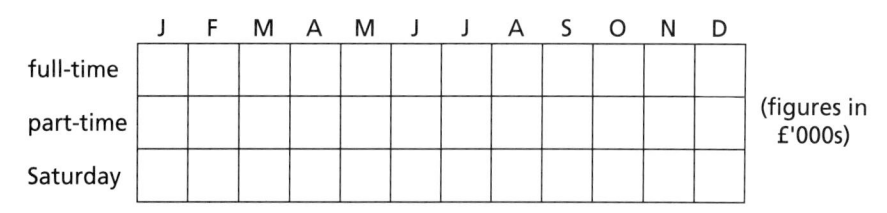

	J	F	M	A	M	J	J	A	S	O	N	D
full-time												
part-time												
Saturday												

(figures in £'000s)

(b) Revenue targets for reservations operators by month

FIGURE 2.6 *(a) Graph and (b) table for use with Task 3*

budget for the year. You may need to revise your calculations if you go over the limit!
- Explain your proposed scheme in your memo, clearly setting out your calculations and including copies of your dispersal diagram and revenue targets table

CHECKLIST OF PORTFOLIO EVIDENCE

- ☑ Completed memo and copies of Figures 2.6(a) and (b).
- ☑ Notes and calculations used in formulating proposals.

SECTION 3

Square Pegs into Square Holes – Recruitment and Selection

Key Aims

This section will help you to:

- understand recruitment and selection procedures used in the leisure and tourism industries
- appreciate the legal and ethical obligations involved in recruiting staff
- evaluate job descriptions and person specifications
- complete application forms, devise a CV and write letters of application
- practise and evaluate interview techniques in preparation for the real thing!

CHOOSING THE BEST PERSON FOR THE JOB

As a leisure and tourism student, it is likely you are a prospective applicant for employment in your chosen field. Your chances of a successful start to your career will be strengthened greatly if you can appreciate the employer's needs and expectations when investing in new staff, as well as your own.

Recruiting staff offers an employer the potential to improve the organisation's performance through the right appointment. Small wonder therefore, that considerable time and effort can be expended on the various stages of the recruitment and selection process (Figure 3.1).

SQUARE PEGS INTO SQUARE HOLES – RECRUITMENT AND SELECTION

```
SKILLS ANALYSIS ── What are the current and future skill requirements
                └─ Develop job description(s) and person specifications
       ↓
Recruitment agencies ─┐
Job centres ──────────┤ ADVERTISE POST(S) ── Newspapers
Careers service ──────┘                   ├─ Specialist trade journals
                                          ├─ Local radio
       ↓                                  └─ Teletext
SEND OUT APPLICATION FORMS ── With job description and personnel specification form
-------- Closing date --------
       ↓
SHORT-LIST APPLICANTS ── Match applicants to personnel specification form
       ↓
INTERVIEW
       ↓
TAKE DECISION
   ↙       ↘
SEND OUT    INFORM SUCCESSFUL ── Venue
REJECTION   APPLICANT(S)      ├─ Start date
LETTERS                       ├─ Contractual details
                              └─ Person to report to on day one
              ↓
          INDUCTION
```

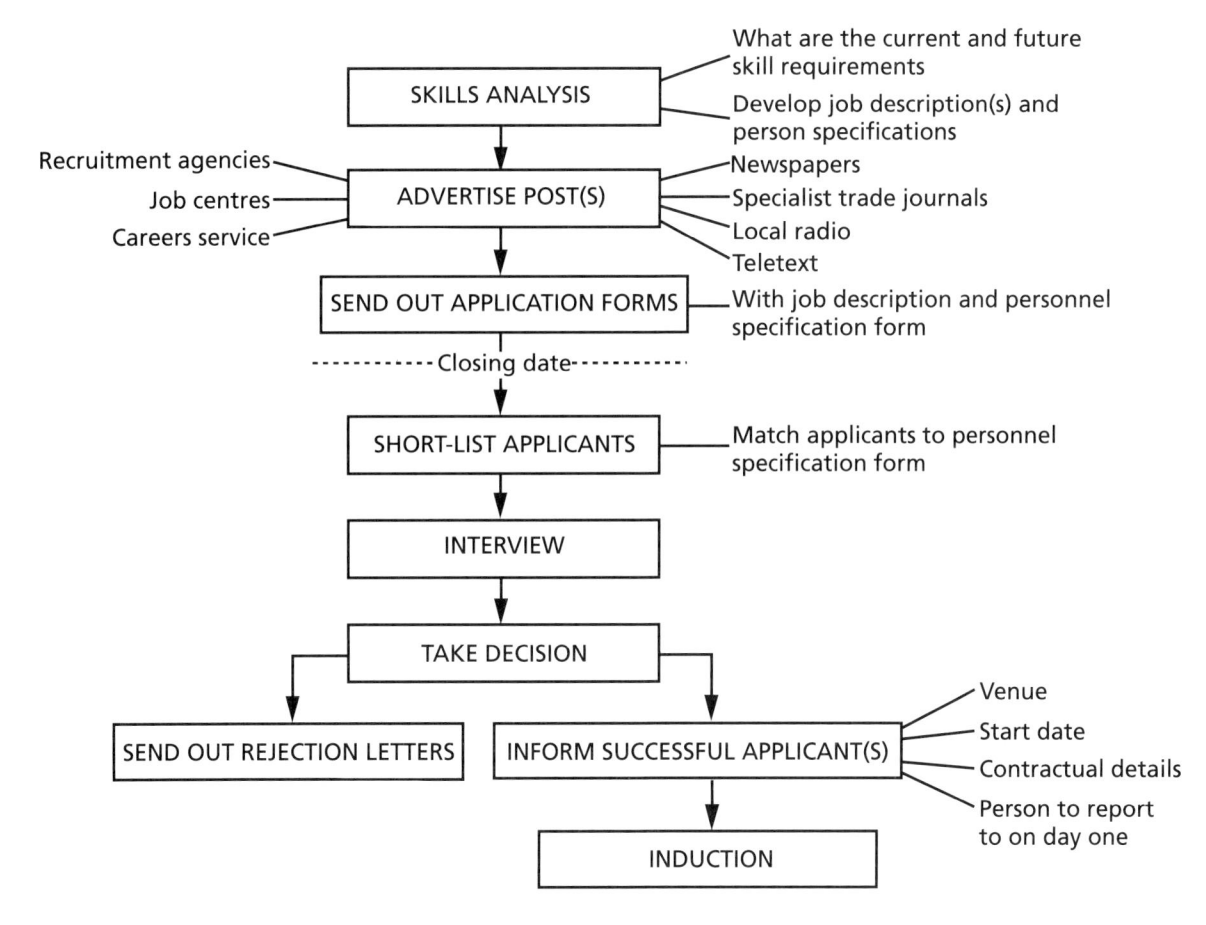

FIGURE 3.1 *The recruitment and selection process*

PANORAMA HOLIDAY GROUP: RECRUITING AND SELECTING OVERSEAS REPRESENTATIVES

The procedures listed in Figure 3.1 are best explored by reference to the recruitment and selection process for one post – that of a Panorama holiday representative. Although not all aspects of this case study will be typical of other leisure and tourism organisations, the essential steps followed by applicant and employer in seeking and finding a suitable job/employee are clearly evident.

Could you work as a holiday representative? You will be asked to apply for such a vacancy as part of Task 4! The job requires huge amounts of energy and patience, a sense of humour and the ability to deal with all types of people. The representative has a key role in ensuring clients enjoy their holiday.

How does a tour operator like Panorama find and appoint its representatives?

Skills analysis

Before advertising a post, it is essential that the organisation identifies the skills and abilities it requires in the new appointment. Auditing the present skills within the workforce against future needs is a key aspect of HRM. Any shortfall may be met by further training of existing staff or the appointment of new personnel. Such an analysis forms the basis for the drawing up of a **job description** and **person specification** for a new post.

The job description should provide an accurate outline of the major duties involved in the position, the salary or grade, the responsibilities of the post and who the holder is accountable to. An alternative

FIGURE 3.2 *Panorama holiday reps at work*

approach is to specify the outcomes expected, reflecting the occupational standards embodied in the position (see Section 4 for more details).

Job descriptions may need alteration as the nature of the job evolves. A job description is best seen as a working document that tells both employee and employer the who? what? why? how? where? and when? of the post.

The person specification details the attributes, qualities, achievements, competencies and qualifications seen as ideal in the successful applicant. A checklist of *selection criteria* can be devised as a result against which applications can be measured. Certain criteria may be ranked as essential to the post, others as desirable.

Panorama sends a leaflet *working overseas with Panorama* and an application form in response to all job enquiries. Extracts from the leaflet are given in Figure 3.3, including details of three overseas posts. The details are simple job descriptions and person specifications. They briefly describe the duties expected of each post and the broad selection criteria to be applied to candidates. More detailed job descriptions will be agreed on appointment.

Advertising vacancies

The job descriptions and person specifications devised for a vacancy will provide the main details of the job advertisement. Employers may advertise vacancies through a variety of channels dependent upon the nature of the post and the applicants they hope to attract:

- the Careers Service, Job centres or recruitment agencies will hold details of vacancies in the local area
- *situations vacant* advertisements in local, regional or national newspapers
- local radio or teletext advertisements
- trade journals and papers such as *Travel Trade Gazette, The Caterer and Hotelkeeper, Local Government Opportunities, Museums Bulletin* and *Leisure Opportunities*.

Panorama rarely advertise overseas posts as they receive a constant flow of general enquiries for overseas work. It is important to realise therefore that employers may expect applicants to take the initiative of enquiring about vacancies, rather than wait for posts to be advertised.

Short-listing applicants

Applicants for Panorama representative positions are asked to submit a completed application form, supported by a letter of application and CV. These are perused by the Overseas manager and other staff prior to short-listing suitable applicants for interview.

The format of the application form (Figure 3.4) is consistent with those of many other organisations. It includes a self-appraisal matrix in which the applicant is asked to rate a range of his/her skills and abilities. A completed matrix scoring 'very good' in all categories tends to raise eyebrows of suspicion, rather than of admiration! One criterion that is rated as highly important by the company for a representative's position, is punctuality – an applicant who rates their own timekeeping as 'fair' or worse is unlikely to be short-listed.

The information gleaned from the application form, accompanying letter and CV is matched against the person specifications of the post. Formal qualifications expected are four good GCSE passes (maths, geography and drama rate highly) or Intermediate GNVQ, although many applicants offer advanced qualifications.

Experience of working in leisure and tourism or with people in general; evidence of having lived away from home; the flexibility to work in different countries; language skills and a clean driving licence are all significant pluses in an application that may lead to the offer of an interview.

Interviews

Interviews for Panorama representatives' vacancies are led by a panel of three

working overseas with...

PANORAMA

Thank you for your enquiry regarding employment overseas with our company. Panorama Holiday Group Limited, comprises of several specialist brochures featuring holidays to Spain, Tunisia with an individual Golf programme, and ski holidays to Andorra and Italy. We also own two retail travel agents the Brighton Travel Shop as well as the Hove Travel Shop.

We are looking for staff to join our overseas team to help us maintain first class standards of service, and enhance the excellent reputation we have within the travel industry.

You will only be suitable for this kind of work if you are patient, calm, flexible, have an outgoing personality, enjoy dealing with all types of people as well as having plenty of common sense and stamina.

We like to think of our overseas representatives as ambassadors for our company. Your role is the key to our success, as you are the only members of our staff customers meet. All applicants who are accepted at the interview stage, have to then attend our training course which will cover all areas of a representatives job. Upon successful completion a position will be offered within our overseas programme.

If selected you may be required to provide a medical certificate, stating there is no reason why you should not work overseas.

If you are interested in a position with our company overseas, the following pages describe the various posts which make up our overseas team.

Panorama Holiday Group interview and employ staff overseas each year. If you are selected you will be paid by the Panorama Holiday Group, tax and NI deductions will be made from your gross salary. If you are a non UK resident, tax and social security payments in the country concerned are the responsibility of the applicant and no deductions will be made by the Panorama Holiday Group. (Overseas salaries are not high).

Employment offered is seasonal and dependent on the level of bookings and other factors.

AREA MANAGER
The main link between overseas and our Brighton office. Responsible for the day to day running of our resorts, the manager ensures our high standards are met in all areas. Their responsibilities include accounts, transfers, quality control, personnel management, as well as public relations. The manager controls our overseas operation.

Requirements:-
* Must be aged over 27 years
* Experience of working as Senior Representative or Area Manager
* Excellent organisational skills
* Clean driving licence
* Good knowledge of accounts
* Total flexibility, willing to work in a resort of our choice and be moved if necessary
* Leadership qualities
* A sense of humour
* Good knowledge of either French, Spanish, Arabic or Italian

OVERSEAS REPRESENTATIVE
The frontline of our overseas operation dealing directly with guests. Duties include coach transfers, welcome meetings and welcome tours, guiding excursions to places of interest and looking after the general welfare of our guests, to make their holiday the most memorable and enjoyable ever.

Requirements:-
* Must be aged over 21 years
* Well presented at all times
* Total flexibility, willing to work in a resort of our choice and be moved if necessary
* A European language is beneficial
* A good level of literacy and numeracy
* Common sense
* Able to communicate at all levels
* Outgoing personality
* Plenty of stamina

CHILDREN'S REPRESENTATIVE
Responsible for the running of our children's club called the Sandcastle Club for 3–11 year olds, whilst parents take a well deserved break. The Sandcastle Club organises games and activities to keep the children amused and having fun 4–6 hours per day. Babysitting duties will also be a part of your job.

Requirements:-
* Must be aged over 20 years
* Well presented at all times
* Total flexibility, willing to work in a resort of our choice and be moved if necessary
* NNEB qualified or similar
* A good level of literacy and numeracy
* Common sense
* Able to communicate at all levels
* Outgoing personality
* Plenty of stamina

FIGURE 3.3 *Extracts from information leaflet* working overseas with Panorama

PANORAMA

APPLICATION FOR EMPLOYMENT

Position applied for _____

THE INFORMATION BELOW IS CONFIDENTIAL.
IT WILL BE USED BY THE COMPANY FOR EMPLOYMENT PURPOSES ONLY.
PLEASE USE BLOCK CAPITALS AND COMPLETE ALL SECTIONS FULLY

photo affix here

Surname _____

First Names _____

Place of Birth _____ Nationality _____ N.I. No. _____

Date of Birth _____ Age _____ Male ☐ Female ☐

EC Passport No. _____ Issued at _____ Expiry Date _____

Contact Address _____

Daytime Tel. _____ Evening Tel. _____

Address of next of kin _____

Would you be prepared to work in any resort within our programme? Yes ☐ No ☐

If no, please state the relevant countries with your reasons _____

Are you available to work either or both of the following periods without any visits home?

Summer Season: April to October Yes ☐ No ☐ **Winter Season** Yes ☐ No ☐

If no, please state dates available and why _____

What is your most convenient UK airport? 1. _____ 2. _____

Do you hold a Full Driving Licence? Yes ☐ No ☐ Date of issue _____

Would you be prepared to drive overseas? Yes ☐ No ☐

FIGURE 3.4 *Panorama application form for an overseas post*

Please state where you heard about Panorama _____

Have you ever worked for Panorama before? Yes ☐ No ☐

If yes, please give details _____

Please tick where appropriate

Do you?   Swim ☐   Smoke ☐   Height _____ Weight _____

If you are applying for the Winter Ski season, please answer the following questions

Can you ski?   Yes ☐ No ☐   No. of weeks ski experience _____

What is your level of ability?   Beginner ☐ Intermediate ☐ Advanced ☐

Please state if you have any qualifications in ski instruction _____

Please give details of your current or most recent employment and your two previous positions

Position held _____

Name and address of employer _____

_____

Start date _____ Date left _____ Salary _____

Reason for leaving _____

Position held _____ Reason for leaving _____

Name and address of employer _____

_____

Start date _____ Date left _____ Salary _____

Position held _____ Reason for leaving _____

Name and address of employer _____

_____

Start date _____ Date left _____ Salary _____

FIGURE 3.4 *continued*

Education History

Please start with the most recent, including both academic and vocational qualifications, e.g. Childcare, Catering, First Aid.

Place of education	From	To	Subjects	Level	Grade

Languages/Skills

	In speaking					In understanding					In reading				
	a Very good	b Good	c Fair	d Poor	e No ability	a Very good	b Good	c Fair	d Poor	e No ability	a Very good	b Good	c Fair	d Poor	e No ability
Spanish															
French															
Arabic															
Italian															
Other															

Abilities in:	a Very good	b Good	c Fair	d Poor	e No ability	Abilities in:	a Very good	b Good	c Fair	d Poor	e No ability
First-aid						Leadership					
Typing/Computing						Organisation					
Accounting						Punctuality					
Selling						Entertaining					
Sales-technique						Creative thinking					
Public speaking						Logical thinking					

Hobbies/Interests _____

FIGURE 3.4 *continued*

Please give details of any diagnosed medical condition _____

_____

Why would you like to work on our overseas programme? _____

_____

_____

What qualities do you feel that you have to become a good overseas team member?

_____

_____

Please describe a recent achievement of which you are particularly proud and outline why

_____

_____

_____

Please give two references including current or most recent employer

Name _____   Name _____

Address _____   Address _____

_____   _____

Title _____   Title _____

If you wish to include any additional information that you feel may assist your application, please write your comments on a blank piece of paper and attach to your application. We are unable to return any documents or photographs.

I declare that the information given on this application form is accurate. I understand that if any information is found to be incorrect my application may be rejected or my employment terminated forthwith.

Signature _____   Date _____

Please note the the applicant is responsible for all travelling expenses to attend interview.

FIGURE 3.4 *continued*

management staff. The process lasts approximately three hours and is made up of a variety of activities:

- group interviews of six to eight applicants in which each is asked to give a short presentation on a pre-arranged topic
- case study questions in groups. These present the applicants with common situations and problems faced by reps
- written tests in Maths, languages and skiing knowledge (where relevant)
- formal one to one interviews which focus on details given in CVs and application forms or arising from the two references taken up by the company on each applicant

The use of a combination of group interviews, simulations, assessment and formal interviews is widespread amongst employers. Certain candidates may perform well or badly in formal situations – other selection procedures help give a wide-ranging picture of each applicant and reveal inter-personal skills or attributes not readily evident in one to one interviews. Psychometric or personality tests are commonplace in successful Japanese companies and are now used by over 75 per cent of all UK companies with more than 1,000 employees. The tests help identify the key attributes many employers are looking for – not least an ability to learn, to adapt and a commitment to the employer.

One further procedure used in interviews is the work sample – this may take the form of observation of each applicant performing an actual task, or referring to evidence of previous work such as Records of Achievement or GNVQ Portfolios of Evidence.

Confirming employment and notifying rejection

Candidates for Panorama representatives vacancies are informed of the decision of the interviewing panel by post within two weeks. Successful applicants are not offered an immediate position as a representative, but are invited to a week's training course in Majorca, the successful completion of which will lead to a job offer (see Section 4). The formal job offer letter is an important document as it will form the basis for the contract of employment (see page 34).

With strong competition for employment, there will usually be more losers than winners in interviews. Rejected applicants should not be forgotten however. They too deserve the courtesy of a letter informing them of the decision made. This helps maintain a good image of the organisation. The letter might give positive feedback on why the candidate was not suitable, so he or she could address these points in future applications.

LEGAL AND ETHICAL OBLIGATIONS

The recruitment and selection process can be fraught with difficulties if correct procedures are not adhered to. Certain legal considerations must be borne in mind which, if not followed, could result in prosecution. There are also moral or ethical issues underpinning the process, such as the need for mutual honesty and objectivity on the parts of both interviewer and applicant.

Equal opportunities

Treating people fairly according to their individual needs is the central aim of equal opportunities policies within organisations. By law, recruitment and employment should be free from prejudice and discrimination.

It is important these two terms are understood clearly. Prejudice involves making a judgement based on subjective feelings and without the reasoned, objective use of facts. Discrimination involves acting as a result of prejudice, for example in refusing someone a job because of the bias felt towards him or her. Discrimination may be *direct*, such as advertising a vacancy for a specific gender, or *indirect*, for example advertising a vacancy only for people over 6ft, thus excluding the majority of women in favour of taller men.

Discrimination is permissible if employers

can show proof of *genuine occupational qualification* (GOQ). For example, the owners of an Indian restaurant could claim that only Indian staff should be recruited to preserve the authenticity of the service provided. The stated requirement for female staff in a sports centre would also be acceptable where access to female changing rooms was an essential part of the job role.

Legislation to combat different forms of discrimination includes:

- The Equal Pay Act 1970 (amended in 1983) – gives workers the right to equal pay for work of equal value. This is particularly relevant in comparing pay for like work between men and women. During the past decade women's average hourly earnings have still remained at around 74 per cent of men's.
- The Sex Discrimination Act 1975 prohibits discrimination and harassment on the grounds of gender. The Act applies to recruitment, promotion and the behaviour of other employees as well as the employer. The Equal Opportunities Commission (EOC) was established under the Act to devise codes of practice towards the elimination of sex discrimination.
- The Race Relations Act 1976 applies the same basic principles to the elimination of race discrimination and created the Commission for Racial Equality (CRE). Addresses for both the EOC and CRE are given on page 57
- The Employment Protection (Consolidation) Act 1978 gives pregnant women the rights not to be dismissed; to time off for antenatal care; to maternity pay and to return to work. There is no statutory right at present to paternity leave or parental leave for sick children in the UK however
- The Disabled Persons (Employment) Acts 1944 and 1958 include the stipulation that employers of more than 20 staff are required to employ registered disabled persons for at least three per cent of their workforce. The Disabled Persons Act 1981 introduced measures requiring employers to provide for access and mobility for disabled people within the workplace
- The Trade Union and Labour Relations (Consolidation) Act 1992 prohibits the restriction of employment to someone who is or is not a member of a particular trade union

At present discrimination according to age is not outlawed. Although some employers have recently changed policies to welcome older recruits, a survey of job advertisements in any national newspaper will provide ready evidence of cut-off ages of 40 or 45 for many posts.

The contract of employment

Employers and employees will both benefit from a clear written statement of the terms and conditions of employment as potential for subsequent confusion and dispute over work practices should be reduced. The Employment Protection (Consolidation) Act 1978 requires employers to provide a written contract for:

- employees working 16 hours or more per week within 13 weeks of taking up a post (reduced to two months under the Trade Union Reform and Employment Rights Act 1993)
- employees working between 8 to 16 hours per week within five years of starting in the post

All workers also have the legal right to a formal letter of acceptance of employment containing: a firm offer of work, the hours of work linked to the post, the standard opening and closing times of the organisation and the start date, time and contact name to report to.

A worker's contract of employment must include the following details:

- the names of employer and employee
- the start date of employment
- the job title
- payment details – the wage, payment intervals and how pay is calculated

- hours of work – the contract should state the basic hours to be worked and on which days, although some contracts may include annual rather than weekly totals, or allow flexible working hours within a given daily range – certain jobs, e.g. cabin crew and pilots, have legal restrictions on working hours
- holiday entitlement and pay (including public holidays) – virtually no workers in the UK are legally entitled to holiday leave and pay however
- pension conditions
- conditions applying to sickness, injuries and sick pay
- the length of notice required of both employee and employer on terminating the contract
- details of disciplinary and grievance procedures (see Section 4)

In addition to the expressed terms given above, a contract can also be seen to contain unwritten implied terms. These would include the need for both parties to act in a way that ensures the health and safety of workers and clients, for example. Contractual disputes brought to **industrial tribunals** often focus on the implied terms of a contract in determining realistic expectations as to the exact duties to be undertaken in a given job.

Contracts of employment differ in their permanency. A permanent contract is a continuous arrangement with no closing date until notice is given either by employer or employee. A temporary contract extends for a finite period only. Temporary contracts are commonplace for seasonal work in leisure and tourism, and increasingly popular in other organisations anxious to curb wage bills. Employees on temporary contracts should seek the same rights and conditions as colleagues on permanent contracts however. Subcontracts involve the employment of specialist staff for a limited period. The growth of CCT has led to companies tendering for subcontracts to provide services in private and public sector leisure and tourism facilities.

Key Skills Hint: Communication

Application forms, CVs and letters of application.

Making a good impression on paper may be the difference between finishing the recruitment and selection race and falling at the first hurdle. Read Figure 3.5 to identify common mistakes made by job applicants.

Employment / own goal by applicants

Illiterate CVs from graduates put them straight on scrapheap

By Judith Judd
Education Editor

EMPLOYERS: do you want communicatory dexterities or proactive action? Then turn to Britain's graduates. Their failure to spell correctly, use plain English or give intelligent answers to simple questions are revealed in a trawl through recent applications carried out by a management consultancy. Some even send in their CVs on Snoopy notepaper.

If growing numbers of them are having to take low-grade jobs, as a recent survey shows, then that, to judge from the CVs sent to the Lewis Consulting Group, may be exactly what they deserve.

The group in Covent Garden, London advertises for bright, energetic business graduates with one or two foreign languages who should have either an upper second or a first class degree.

The latest batch of 100 CVs sent to the firm, which takes on three or four graduates a year, shows that graduates do not believe in using one word where four or five will do.

"I am," says one applicant, "most confident in my communicatory dexterities." "I have experience," says another, "of pro-active action on issues of concern."

A survey by the National Institute for Economic and Social Research last month showed that almost half of graduates employed by banks and building societies have to take low-grade jobs. Chris Lewis, the Lewis group's managing director, says: "This is no real shock to employers when so many graduate CVs appear to have been written by creatures from the planet errata."

One CV sent to him contained 14 spelling mistakes. "I have had a plethora of travelling experiances," or "My interessests include the challange of overseas travel," are typical. Other spelling errors include persuit, genoration and envolvment.

The person who took up a position as a minicab driver (sic) and the one with excellent writing (sic) skills were presumably just being careless. Some even sent the first half of the letter addressed to one firm along with the second half directed at another. One letter to the Lewis group began "Dear Linda" because it was meant for a travel firm. Another said simply "Dear Lewis".

Mr Lewis, whose group receives several hundred applications from graduates each year, says: "Ninety-five per cent of our applicants don't even get an interview because their CVs are so appalling. These people may well have the skills we need but they don't know how to do justice to themselves."

Even those who reach the interview stage are often inept at handling questions. One phone conversation went like this:

Mr Lewis: "Hello, I wanted to chat with you for two minutes about a recent application you made for our graduate recruitment programme."

Applicant: "Can you call back? I'm just about to have a bath."

Or "What's your long-term ambition?" Answer: "To get some quick work experience and move on."

Mr Lewis says: "Whatever universities are teaching students, they are not getting the message across on CVs and job applications. They're generally unchecked, often brief and never followed up. Students are not being coached through the application process."

It is not surprising, he adds, that some students apply for 200 jobs and receive no reply. "Understandably many employers can't be bothered to respond to applicants who not read either the brief for the job or their own CV."

A survey of employers last week showed that graduates' employment prospects are improving. Job vacancies are up 17.5 per cent.

But Mr Lewis believes that big increases in vacancies will not help some graduates and that graduate unemployment will continue for some time. Good employers will refuse to jeopardise their business by taking on poor quality trainees.

Independent on Sunday 2-7-95

FIGURE 3.5 *Illiterate CVs from graduates put them straight on scrapheap*
SOURCE: The Independent on Sunday 2 July 1995

Completing application forms

- Draft your answers on a copy of the form before completing your final version
- Follow instructions on the form to the letter, e.g. answering in block capitals where requested. Complete the form even if the information required is duplicated on your enclosed CV – Panorama reject all incomplete application forms, for instance, as the opening instructions to complete the form fully have not been followed!
- Complete the form in blue or black ink for ease of photocopying by both you and the employer. Refer to your copy to refresh your memory if you are called for interview
- Don't leave gaps on the application form where something does not apply to you – write N/A (not applicable) to show you have not overlooked the question
- Check the completed form is well presented. Look up all words that you are not sure of spelling correctly
- Answer questions fully, giving as much detail of your interests and achievements as possible. Don't sell yourself short!

Compiling your CV

CV stands for *curriculum vitae*, Latin for 'course of one's life'. It is an individual document, unique to yourself. As such, you should decide on its exact format and contents. Figure 3.6 is a CV template which can be adapted to suit you. Guidelines for a good CV include:

- word process or desktop publish your CV so that it can be updated and printed as required
- keep your CV to one or two sides only. Use bullet points to transmit information concisely
- your CV is a marketing promotion selling you! It must be clear and attractive to the reader. Make headings stand out and follow a logical sequence
- set your CV apart from the others through, for example, an attractive design, presenting it in a transparent folder, or by enclosing an action photograph of yourself!
- don't simply describe the jobs you have undertaken in the past, but stress the skills you developed performing them, which a new employer would benefit from
- don't forget a covering letter of application to accompany your CV (see below)

Writing letters of application

The letter of application will usually accompany your CV and/or application form. It will be the first thing an employer will read, so must make a good impression. Letters may vary in format according to the job advertisement. An advert asking you to apply in writing will require a detailed letter. An advert asking you to write for further details and an application form requires a concise response, as you will give fuller information when you return your completed application.

- Should you write or word process your letter? Employers' preferences vary widely. Job adverts may state that you should apply in your own handwriting, in this case the decision is made for you. Otherwise, you must judge the best way to present your application as attractively as possible
- If writing your letter, ensure there are no mistakes or alterations – write the letter again if you have had to make corrections
- Structure your letter carefully. Name the job applied for, giving its reference code if mentioned in the advert and where you saw the advert. State why you want the post – describe positive aspects of the organisation, its staff and the challenge of the job. Say why you think you should get the job – link the skills and experience outlined in your CV to those required in the advert
- Start and finish your letter correctly – 'Dear Sir' should end 'Yours faithfully', and 'Dear Ms Smith' should be signed 'Yours sincerely'. Print your name after your signature. Include your address and telephone number (and fax number if available)

Curriculum Vitae

Personal

Surname

Forename(s)

Address/Telephone Number

Date of birth/Age

Marital status

Personal statement/profile – *describe your strengths and skills – use concrete examples to show potential employers what you are capable of. You may choose to place this section at the end of your CV.*

Education

Current school/college – *include dates attended and any posts of responsibility.*

Previous secondary school/college *(if applicable – include dates).*

Current courses studied – *include predicted grades if known.*

Qualifications – *in chronological order – latest first – group high grades together so they are more prominent.*

Employment

Include full-time, part-time and work experience – use bullet points to describe your position and duties and the skills you developed as a result – give start and finish dates.

Interests

Use this section to illustrate your skills and abilities – e.g. team sports indicate the ability to work in a team. Include interests and hobbies both inside and outside of school/college. Add details of posts of responsibility and awards and qualifications e.g. first aid certificate.

Referees

Supply names and addresses of two people who know you well – one should be your school headteacher/college principal. Make sure you have asked their permission to be used as referees.

FIGURE 3.6 *A CV template*

Key Skills Hint: Communication

Job interview techniques

The following checklist suggests points to remember in the roles of both interviewer and interviewee.

The interviewer

- Plan the questions you wish to ask, but be flexible in the manner and order you ask your questions in response to the candidate's answers – effective listening allows you to help the candidate to contribute and makes for successful interviews
- Begin with one or two ice breaker questions to put the candidate at ease
- Take notes during the interview so that you can make informed decisions later – you may confuse candidates' details after several interviews if you only rely on your memory
- Ask open rather than closed questions that encourage the candidates to talk about themselves
- Do not ask questions that could be interpreted as prejudiced – think to yourself 'would I ask the same question to a man/white person/able-bodied person?' – try to ask the same questions to all candidates
- Use encouraging body language and check the environment of the room – the lighting, seating etc. – is welcoming rather than threatening
- Give candidates the chance to answer fully and ask their own questions
- Avoid asking several questions at the same time or the use of confusing jargon
- Probe a candidate's answers for depth of knowledge and summarise their responses to check you have understood them
- Ask each candidate if they are still interested in the post at the end of the interview – they may have changed their minds!
- Don't be concerned if you fail to appoint at an interview – it proves you have employed rigorous selection procedures!

The interviewee

- Preparation is essential: check the time, date and travel arrangements for the interview – confirm in writing you will be attending – find out what you can about the organisation – consider which aspects of your course you can talk about: work experience, planning an event, best assignments etc. – decide on any work sample documents you will take – plan questions you will ask at the interview
- Ensure your appearance is well-groomed and clothes are clean and neatly ironed
- First impressions count: introduce yourself confidently and cheerfully, be prepared to knock and enter the interview room and shake hands, but don't sit until offered a chair
- Think about your body language and maintaining eye contact with the interviewer – but not to the point of fixed staring or sitting rigidly in one position!
- Ensure you know the interviewer's name and use it – listen carefully to questions and watch for audible or visual signals from interviewers to your answers
- Project your talents, achievements and ambitions – impress the interviewer with what you can bring to his/her organisation – but be honest at all times
- Try to relax! – a good interviewer will expect nerves and try to put you at ease
- Be polite to all members of the organisation before, during and after the interview – don't forget to thank the interviewer when you leave
- If you fail to get the job, find out why – ask for constructive feedback that would improve your application or interview performance

TASK 4

DESPERATELY SEEKING SELECTION

This task examines the recruitment and selection process from the perspectives of both employer and job applicant. You are asked to work within a group to shortlist each other's job applications and conduct job interviews.

To complete the task you will need to prepare:

- a full CV
- a completed application form for the post of Overseas Representative with Panorama Holiday Group (use Figure 3.4 as a guide)
- a covering letter of application for the post – assume the minimum age required to be 18 for the sake of this exercise
- a letter of application, CV (and completed application form if available) for one leisure and recreation post chosen by your group as a whole. The job description and person specification details may be for a job at the case study used in Tasks 1 and 2

You should practise your interviewing skills, both as interviewer and interviewee, before undertaking part 3 of the task.

1 Recruitment and selection checklist

dealing with references

confirming employment

shortlisting applicants

dealing with Records of Achievement

notifying rejection

advertising vacancies

assessing applicants

interviews

- The recruitment and selection procedures above are jumbled out of sequence. List them in the order you would expect them to occur in the left hand column of a table organised with the following headings:

Procedure	Explanatory notes	Legal and ethical obligations

- Use the Panorama case study and your own research to (i) add further details of each procedure in the Explanatory notes column and (ii) illustrate the legal and ethical obligations that may be relevant to one or more procedures in the remaining columns

2 Shortlisting applicants for interview

- Analyse the job descriptions and person specifications for a Panorama overseas representative (Figure 3.3) and your chosen leisure and recreation post in turn. Write a brief summary of the extent to which the details of each job:
  - facilitate the matching of applicants to each vacancy
  - minimise the risk of making an inappropriate appointment
  - reflect the objectives of the organisation
  - recognise the potential for training and career progression
- Work in a group of four or five to identify the key features within the job description/person specification of each post. These will be your selection criteria to use in shortlisting applicants for each vacancy. Make your own copies of Figure 3.7 and list your selection criteria under the subheadings given, using a separate copy for each vacancy
- Discuss the applications and CVs of each member of your group for each post. Use your copies of Figure 3.7 to systematically evaluate each application against your selection criteria
- Decide as a group which two applicants you would shortlist for interview for each of the two vacancies. Add accompanying notes to support your decision to interview or reject each applicant.

3 Interviewing applicants

- Work with one other student to demonstrate interview techniques for each post. Decide who is to be the interviewer and interviewee for the Panorama post and then swap roles for your chosen leisure and recreation job. The interviewer should review the interviewee's application and CV prior to the interview, prepare questions and plan the framework of the interview
- Use a copy of Figure 3.8 to evaluate your performance in each role. The evaluation can be undertaken by your teacher or lecturer, a local employer or fellow student. The score from 1 to 5, although fairly arbitrary in nature, provides an indication of strengths and weaknesses in your performance. Why not videotape your interviews so that you can also appraise your own performance?

CHECKLIST OF PORTFOLIO EVIDENCE

- ☑ Completed recruitment and selection procedures table.
- ☑ Summaries of analysis of job descriptions/person specifications for both vacancies.
- ☑ Copies of your CV, letters of application and application form(s) for both posts.
- ☑ Two copies of Figure 3.7 with accompanying notes supporting shortlisting decisions.
- ☑ Copy of Figure 3.8 providing records of observation of techniques as interviewer and interviewee.

SHORTLISTING APPLICANTS FOR INTERVIEW

Organisation:
Vacancy:

Selection criteria	Applicants				
	1	2	3	4	5
key job responsibilities – *evidence of experience in similar role?*					
personal attributes *e.g. communication skills*					
personal qualities *e.g. caring nature*					
personal achievements *e.g. sports awards*					
vocational qualifications – *GNVQs, NVQs, BTEC etc*					
academic qualifications – *GCSEs, A levels etc*					
competence *e.g. driving licence*					
assessment of content of application/CV					
quality of presentation of application/CV					
select for interview?	Y N	Y N	Y N	Y N	Y N

FIGURE 3.7 *Shortlisting applicants for interview record sheet*

HUMAN RESOURCES IN LEISURE AND TOURISM

Student name:

Evaluation of role as interviewer

Interview for position of:

	Score 1 (weak) – 5 (excellent)	Comments
Interview framework	☐	
Objective questioning	☐	
Listening skills	☐	
Body language	☐	
Decision-making	☐	

Evaluation of role as interviewee

Interview for position of:

Preparation	☐
Personal presentation	☐
Body language	☐
Question and answer technique	☐
Listening skills	☐
Assertiveness	☐
Confidence	☐

Overall assessment:

FIGURE 3.8 *Interview techniques observation sheet*

SECTION 4

Rules and Regulations – Workplace Standards and Conditions

Key Aims

This section will help you to:

- understand legislation relating to workplace standards and conditions in the leisure and tourism industries
- describe how workplace standards can be maintained
- appreciate the benefits of occupational standards
- use information sources and desk top publishing skills to produce an induction booklet for new staff

JOINING THE ORGANISATION

Figure 4.1 places recruitment and selection with other elements of HRM into a continual system structured around the needs and goals of an enterprise. The assimilation of new staff into the organisation will be followed by a review of their performance at regular intervals. Further training and career development may result in promotion or a new position with a revised job description.

Refer to Figure 3.1 as well as Figure 4.1. Both indicate the recruitment and selection process will be followed by **induction** of the new employee into the organisation. This is a vital period in which staff learn about the policies and procedures of their new employer as well as their rights and responsibilities.

A thorough induction programme should help avoid mistakes and misunderstandings as newcomers find their feet. Many organisa-

The Human Resource Management Cycle

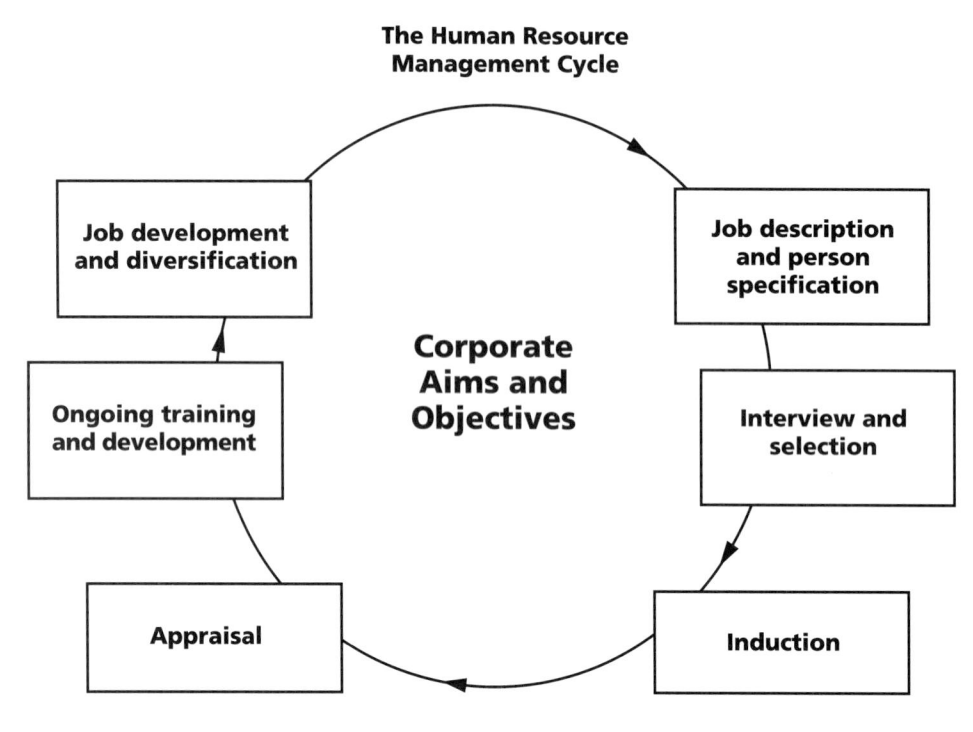

```
        Job development                    Job description
        and diversification                and person
                                           specification
                    ↑
        Ongoing training      Corporate    Interview and
        and development       Aims and     selection
                              Objectives
            Appraisal                      Induction
```

FIGURE 4.1 *The human resource management cycle*

tions issue staff with an induction manual or company handbook as a guide to items such as: health and safety, quality standards, salary, illness and sick pay, leave and holidays, communications, and problems at work. Task 5 asks you to design an induction booklet for Panorama representatives.

Induction for Panorama overseas representatives is in two phrases. A week's training course in Majorca introduces staff to general aspects of their role including welcome meetings, airport transfers, booking excursions and health and safety. Having successfully completed the week, the new representatives are then allocated to their resort and spend a period of time before the arrival of the first guests familiarising themselves with the area, the excursions and local staff and procedures.

WORKPLACE LEGISLATION

Leisure and tourism organisations are subject to a range of UK and EU laws and directives focusing upon standards and conditions in the workplace. This legislation seeks to prevent harmful or serious incidents by enforcing guidelines and procedures to protect employers, employees and clients.

Legal rights of employers and employees

Section 3 has examined many of the legal obligations of employment. An extended checklist of employer and employee's rights under the law includes:

- freedom from discrimination in recruitment or employment on the grounds of race, gender or marital status
- a written statement of the terms and conditions of employment within the first two months of commencing a job
- safe working conditions to minimum national standards
- freedom from discrimination on the grounds of trade union membership

RULES AND REGULATIONS – WORKPLACE STANDARDS AND CONDITIONS

- the right to full payment on the agreed dates
- for women, not to be dismissed on grounds of pregnancy and to be granted maternity leave
- to be able to return to work after illness
- not to be unfairly dismissed. The Employment Protection Act 1978, amended by the Employment Act 1989, protects employees against unfair **dismissal**. In practice, fair and reasonable dismissal will be due to either: an employee's misconduct, lack of capability in the job role or **redundancy**. Employers will be expected by industrial tribunals to back their decisions with documentary evidence and to show they have given the employee clear notification of their intentions and expectations
- employees must be given a written explanation when dismissed. They may not claim unfair dismissal however if (a) over the retirement age (b) work less than 16 hours per week or (c) have worked for an organisation for less than two years. Should a tribunal find for an employee, they may be reinstated in their job, re-engaged in a similar job or paid compensation
- the right to a lump sum of money if made redundant after two years continuous service with an employer, having worked over 16 hours per week and aged between 18 and 65. Employers must inform relevant trade unions and employees of proposed redundancies in writing, detailing: reasons for the redundancies; numbers and jobs of employees affected; how and when redundancies will be selected

ACAS, the Advisory, Conciliation and Arbitration Service, is a government-appointed body set up in 1970 to act as a third party in settling industrial disputes and grievances. The ACAS council is composed of representatives from employers and trade unions. ACAS issues codes of practice to guide employers, employees and trade unions in employment procedures and offers free advice to individuals or organisations.

Cause for concern – issues of discipline and grievance

Disagreements or problems between employer and employee may arise on occasions. A concern or complaint of an employee towards his or her organisation is termed a grievance. Employers unhappy at the standards of work, behaviour or attendance may feel the need to discipline an employee. If matters cannot be settled informally, organisations have developed formal disciplinary and grievance procedures. Figure 4.2 on page 48 is an example of how these might be dealt with in a company handbook.

As in the grievance process, disciplinary procedures are usually in four stages:

- Stage One: formal verbal warning
- Stage Two: formal written warning
- Stage Three: final written warning
- Stage Four: dismissal

Examples of gross misconduct, for which dismissal is summary, include:

- theft, fraud or deliberate falsification of records
- fighting or assault on another person
- exposing the company to viruses through loading unauthorised software
- acts of sexual or racial discrimination or harassment
- incapability through the influence of alcohol or illegal drugs

Health and safety legislation

A companion volume in this series *Health, Safety and Security in Leisure and Tourism* examines this topic in detail. For the purposes of Task 5, a list of the main legislation to research for relevant guidelines includes:

- Health and Safety at Work Act 1974 (sections 2, 3, 4, 7 and 33 in accordance with European directive amendments)
- Fire Precautions Act 1971
- Food Hygiene Regulations
- Offices, Shops and Railway Premises Act 1963

- Control of Substances Hazardous to Health (COSHH) Regulations 1988
- Health and Safety (First Aid) Regulations 1981
- Notification of Accidents and Dangerous Occurrences Regulations 1985

Information on health and safety regulations is obtainable from the Health and Safety Executive (HSE) – address on page 57.

Maintaining workplace standards

In 1988 the Audit Commission in its survey of management practices in British industry noted: 'The single most powerful reason why some organisations are consistently more successful than others is that their employees are better trained and more highly motivated than those of their competitors. They must feel that their contribution is valued by the organisation.' Figure 4.1 includes **appraisal** of staff performance as an integral component of HRM. It is one method whereby organisations can focus on the individual development of each employee and monitor standards of performance and behaviour. Such standards may vary from one company to another, but are likely to include:

- attendance
- punctuality
- hygiene, health, safety and security
- presentation in dress and appearance
- acceptable language and behaviour
- dealing with customers – both internal and external
- concern for the environment – in the workplace and on a wider scale

Staff appraisals involve a regular review of an employee's work, usually with the line manager. The appraisal process should allow informal face-to-face discussion with the main points recorded on paper to avoid misunderstanding and for future action. Discussions should focus on:

- the details of the appraisee's job – clarifying the main duties, responsibilities and accountability of the position
- current achievements – what has been done successfully? What has not gone well? What new targets should be set?
- obstacles to achievement – are there factors affecting the employee's performance? These could include lack of resources or work relationships for instance. What can be done to improve performance?
- creating an action plan – this lists the issues identified and agreed by both parties and the next steps to be taken to improve performance and by whom – this may involve clarifying the employee's job description or the provision of further training for example.

Apart from appraisal reports, an organisation will keep a variety of personnel records of the performance of its human resources. These will include details and statistics for individual staff and for the workforce as a whole. Records may be kept on:

- attendance/absenteeism
- sickness/accidents
- salary details including job grade, taxes, pensions and wages
- annual leave entitlements
- past application forms, personal details and references
- disciplinary matters
- performance and appraisal data

Most organisations use computerised personnel records, but smaller companies may retain a manual filing system. In either case, maintaining the security and confidentiality of the sensitive information stored is essential.

Organisations storing computerised (but not manual) records must be registered with the Data Protection Registrar under the terms of the Data Protection Act (1984). The Act lays down clear guidelines on the type and uses of personnel data stored and the need to maintain security of information. Individual employees are entitled, on written request, to have access to all computerised records about themselves, and for these to be corrected or deleted where appropriate.

RULES AND REGULATIONS – WORKPLACE STANDARDS AND CONDITIONS

All organisations require a framework of workplace rules for its staff to operate successfully and safely. Many organisations draw up customer or employee charters detailing the level of services offered to customers and the quality standards expected of staff. These may be expressed as a list of simple dos and don'ts or presented as guidelines staff should follow. Figure 4.3 on page 49, another example of an extract from a company handbook, is an example of the latter approach.

Occupational standards

The establishment of National Occupational Standards was initiated by the government in 1986 in an attempt to develop agreed benchmarks and qualifications that reflected the needs of industry. Standards have since been developed by ILBs (Industrial Lead Bodies) within the leisure and tourism industries in the areas of sport and recreation, management, travel services and hotel and catering. They are reflected in the five levels of NVQs (National Vocational Qualifications) and SVQs (Scottish Vocational Qualifications) which are similar in their structure of units, elements and performance criteria to GNVQs, but have a more specific occupational focus.

What are the benefits of occupational standards?

They can be seen as an attempt to replace a bewildering plethora of vocational qualifications with the national framework of five NVQ/SVQ levels. The standards outline the **competencies** required of personnel at each level and these may then be used as the basis of job descriptions and person specifications. Figure 4.4 illustrates the job description of a recreation assistant in a leisure complex that has been related to NVQ units.

Occupational standards may be utilised by organisations as benchmarks for skills analysis and audits, or as yardsticks against which to conduct staff appraisals or plan training programmes. NVQ/SVQs allow employees to gain recognition for their skills and abilities in the workplace and use their qualifications as a basis for further training or career development. A better qualified workforce should in turn offer a better service to the customer, resulting in a more successful organisation.

The NVQ/SVQ system has been criticised by some as bureaucratic and costly in its assessment procedures. NVQs (with GCSEs, A levels and GNVQs or Applied A levels) are central to the government's National Targets for Education and Training shown in Figure 4.5. They are likely, therefore, to continue to evolve and gain acceptance.

Grievances

We hope you'll be happy in your work but should you have any problems or complaints about your job or conditions of employment, these should be discussed initially with your immediate supervisor or manager. If you are unhappy with the outcome please contact your personnel advisor. Usually problems can be resolved quickly and amicably but, if not, there is a more formal grievance procedure that ensures your complaint will be dealt with fully and fairly.

Grievance Procedure

Stage One

If you have a problem or complaint and you can't agree a satisfactory solution with your immediate supervisor within a reasonable time, you may refer the matter to your manager or department head. A personnel advisor or work colleague from the same location can be present if necessary.

Stage Two

If resolution is not reached, the matter may be referred to a more senior manager. Again, a personnel advisor or work colleague may be present.

Stage Three

Failing resolution, you may appeal in writing to the UK Personnel manager. A work colleague or personnel adviser may be present.

Stage Four

You may appeal to the Personnel director whose decision is final.

Disciplinary Action

Department heads or managers are responsible for ensuring standards are maintained at work. They have to see that their team runs efficiently, that staff members work together and give their best.

Now and again, problems can occur if your conduct, behaviour or performance fail to meet the standards expected by your manager or by the company. In such cases, you are entitled to fair and proper warnings according to our disciplinary procedure which is designed to help and encourage everyone to achieve and maintain standards of conduct, attendance and job performance. In addition, the company will give you reasonable help to reach the standards of performance required

Principles

- All cases will be fully investigated before disciplinary action is taken.

- At every stage in the procedure you will be advised of the nature of the complaint against you and given the opportunity to state your case before any decision is made.

- At all formal stages of the disciplinary procedure you will have the right to be accompanied by a work colleague from the same work location.

- You will not be dismissed for a first breach of discipline except in the case of gross misconduct, when the penalty will be dismissal without notice.

- You will have the right to appeal against any disciplinay penalty imposed as long as the appeal is made in writing within five working days of the disciplinary action being taken.

- The procedure may be implemented at any stage or stages omitted if the alleged misconduct warrants such action.

FIGURE 4.2 *Grievance and disciplinary action: examples of how this might be dealt with in a company handbook*

RULES AND REGULATIONS — WORKPLACE STANDARDS AND CONDITIONS

The way we dress creates a strong impression with our colleagues and visitors to our offices. These can include customers, staff from overseas or other UK offices, suppliers, prospective members of staff, friends or relatives. It is, therefore, important that we promote a smart image of efficiency and professionalism.

This means that although we do not have strict rules about what you wear at work, we do expect you to use discretion and to dress in an appropriate way with sense and moderation. Very casual clothing is therefore not acceptable.

In some departments you might be required to wear the company uniform or to follow a specific dress code.

FIGURE 4.3 *Workplace rules: an example of how these might be dealt with in a company handbook*

Job Description

Unit/Element	Title: Recreation Assistant – Pools and Sports Hall
	Required – competence to:
H3	Maintain the safety of swimming pool users
H2	Contribute to the security, safety and comfort of clients/customers
R3	Provide and maintain equipment for activities
P19	Support the work of a team
	Beneficial – competence to:
IN7	Receive customers and visitors
IN8	Providing information to customers and clients
D31	Assist in preparing an activity

FIGURE 4.4 *A recreation assistant job description written in competence related terms*

NATIONAL TARGETS FOR EDUCATION AND TRAINING

Targets for 2000

Foundation Learning

1. By age 19, 85% of young people to achieve 5 GCSEs at grade C or above, an Intermediate GNVQ or an NVQ level 2.

2. 75% of young people to achieve level 2 competence in communication, numeracy and IT by age 19; and 35% to achieve level 3 competence in these core skills by age 21.

3. By age 21, 60% of young people to achieve 2 GCE A levels, an Advanced GNVQ or an NVQ level 3.

Lifetime Learning

1. 60% of the workforce to be qualified to NVQ level 3, Advanced GNVQ or 2 GCE A level standard.

2. 30% of the workforce to have a vocational, professional, management or academic qualification at NVQ level 4 or above.

3. 70% of all organisations employing 200 or more employees, and 35% of those employing 50 or more, to be recognised as Investors in People.

FIGURE 4.5 *National Targets for Education and Training*

RULES AND REGULATIONS – WORKPLACE STANDARDS AND CONDITIONS

Key Skills Hint: Information Technology

Desktop publishing (DTP)

Desktop publishing with a PC allows you to produce documents that combine text and graphics. With practice, you can design eye-catching posters, leaflets or newsletters, limited only by the capabilities of your DTP software, the quality of your printer and your own imagination!

The following points give a general overview of DTP facilities, you will also need to familiarise yourself with the specific characteristics of the software and hardware you will be using.

DTP packages incorporate the following features:

- *page layout*: this is best planned before text and graphics are entered, not after! Text may be formatted into columns, but you will need to specify the width and spacing of each column by setting column guides on your page. You may also wish to consider the orientation of the page as portrait or landscape; its size, the printer margins that will be set and the number of pages in your document
- *import text*: text may be loaded from word processor files or electronic mail into the DTP program. It can then be re-arranged to fit the page layout required
- *text fonts and style*: a wide range of scaleable fonts are available in DTP programs. These can vary in size to allow you to give emphasis to headings or titles. In addition, a wide range of character and paragraph styles can be selected from the DTP program's style palette. These include indented text, bullet points and borders. Once selected, the particular style characteristics of a document can be defined as a style sheet and applied to other files. Alternatively, the DTP package will contain several ready-made style sheets or templates for common documents such as memos or invoices which can be used or adapted
- *images*: a variety of graphics may be pasted into DTP pages through imported files – just check your DTP program is able to accept the illustrations you wish to import. Diagrams from spreadsheet applications, scanned illustrations or drawings created using specialist graphics packages can be inserted into text at chosen position. The DTP program may also contain a picture library of pre-drawn clip-art, or these can be imported from disk or CD ROM.

Task 5 asks you to desktop publish an induction booklet for Panorama overseas reps. Figure 4.6 illustrates one page from such a booklet written and designed by a leisure and tourism student using a variety of DTP features.

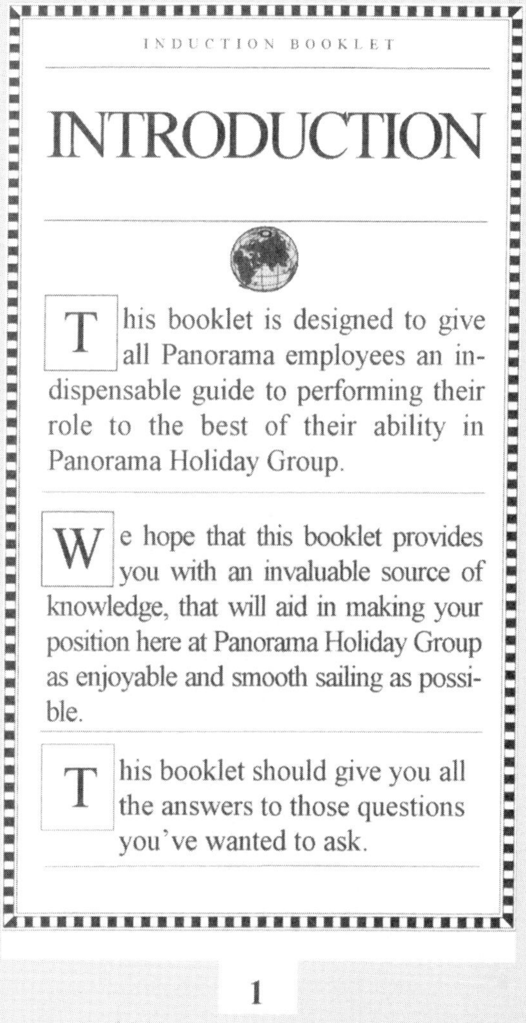

> INDUCTION BOOKLET
>
> # INTRODUCTION
>
> This booklet is designed to give all Panorama employees an indispensable guide to performing their role to the best of their ability in Panorama Holiday Group.
>
> We hope that this booklet provides you with an invaluable source of knowledge, that will aid in making your position here at Panorama Holiday Group as enjoyable and smooth sailing as possible.
>
> This booklet should give you all the answers to those questions you've wanted to ask.
>
> 1

FIGURE 4.6 *A page designed using a DTP package*

TASK 5

SETTING THE STANDARDS

The Panorama overseas representatives' training course in Majorca covers a wide range of workplace duties. Your task is to research, design and desktop publish an induction booklet to accompany key elements of the training course. Possible sources of information include: government departments, the Health and Safety Executive, ACAS, trade unions and trade associations such as ABTA and (at a local level): Training Enterprise Councils, Chambers of Commerce or Citizen's Advice Bureaux. A list of useful addresses is included on page 56.

1 Producing the induction booklet

Your booklet should be made up of three parts.

Part 1 should use short paragraphs, bullet points and illustrations to summarise the purpose of legislation relating to standards and conditions in resorts:

- responsibilities to ensure the health and safety of employees and guests – include some practical guidelines on how to ensure fire safety, gas safety and accommodation hygiene and safety
- employment legislation concerning redundancy, disciplinary procedures and dismissal

Part 2 will focus on standards of performance and behaviour expected of staff:

- quality standards – draw up a 'representative's charter' that outlines the standards representatives should follow regarding: wearing of Panorama uniform, grooming, attendance and timekeeping, attitude to clients, working with other staff, care of the environment
- outline procedures whereby standards of performance and behaviour could be monitored by the company
- provide an introduction to NVQs to inform and encourage representatives to gain these qualifications

Part 3 will be made up of short sample answers to the following scenarios. Your answers should demonstrate the practical, common sense application of some of the guidelines given in Parts 1 and 2.

- A guest approaches you in the hotel reception very distraught as her wedding ring has disappeared from her hotel room whilst she was at breakfast. She is accusing the maid. What action would you take?
- You are sharing an apartment with a fellow representative who is also a good friend. She or he is drinking heavily and staying out all night. As a result her/his work is suffering, for example, s/he is late for hotel visits, forgets to book excursions and so on. What would you do?
- You notice that one of the swings in the hotel playground is damaged. What action would you take?
- An elderly lady falls over in the shower and hurts her arm. What would you do to assist her?

Utilise the capabilities of your DTP package as fully as possible in producing your induction booklet. For example, cartoons or illustrations might enliven certain sections for the reader and help key points stick in the memory. Be sure to acknowledge sources of information you research. The completed booklet should be submitted both as hard copy and on disk.

2 Oral presentation

Prepare a brief presentation that:

- describes the general purpose, procedures and benefits of workplace legislation, standards and conditions within the leisure and tourism industries, using your booklet as an illustration
- details the sources of information and advice relating to workplace standards you have researched
- evaluates the use of the DTP package in the production of your booklet

CHECKLIST OF PORTFOLIO EVIDENCE

- ☑ Completed induction booklet – hard copy and on disk
- ☑ Presentation notes and visual aids

SECTION 5

Review of the Unit

This booklet has sought to promote an insight into human resource management and to generate the evidence indicators required for Unit 2: *Human Resources in the leisure and tourism industries*.

You have studied different types of organisational structure, the influences upon them and the impacts structures can have in turn on how an organisation will operate. The mechanics and benefits of effective teamwork have been examined. You will have picked up pointers on the procedures and expectations involved in applying for employment in leisure and tourism. Finally, you will have gained an insight into the legal and occupational standards and workplace conditions that leisure and tourism staff work within.

By now, the vital role of human resources in leisure and tourism introduced at the start of this booklet should have become increasingly self-evident. The following task asks you to apply your understanding of HRM to a new scenario outlined in Figure 5.1.

Entertainment

Pre-packed fun in the pleasure dome

MARTIN WROE

The tills are ringing like wedding bells in shrink-wrapped green-field entertainment boxes that are ripping the heart out of town centres

IT IS A WET Thursday evening on the edge of Hemel Hempstead and the good folk of Hertfordshire are pleasuring themselves.

They are gathered in the massive, neon-lit shed that is Leisure World: the bowling balls are rumbling down 20 lanes, ten-pins flying; wannabe Torvills are boogeying round the ice-rink; the 10-screen multiplex is packed; and in the bars and restaurants scattered across the 200,000 square foot floorspace of the shed, the tills are ringing like wedding bells. Welcome to the 'Leisure Box', entertainment Nineties-style, all shrink-wrapped and ready to serve.

'We come here two or three times a week,' says Jenny, 21, who works in a building society and is out with her friends. 'We don't bother with the cinema, we just like to hang out.'

In the Hotshots bar, they are hanging out in their hundreds. Crushed gaggles of teenaged and twentysomething girls in micro-minis, lipstick and not much else are shrieking to be heard through the dance beat.

The bar spills on to several sports areas, where the boys — in jeans, spotless white trainers and polo shirts — are bent over pool tables or testing their golf driving on the simulated range. In between the solid gold hits, the DJ — cruder than Castrol GTX and producing twice the effluence — tries to entertain the pleasure-seekers with sub-Club 18–30 lewdities.

'You are politely reminded that Hotshots' atmosphere and entertainment policy may not be suitable for under-18s after 8pm,' a sign gravely warns, reminding patrons that Leisure World is for all the family in the day — but for only some of the family at night.

The aqua-pool has closed for the evening and at the two nightclubs — Visage, for 'happy house and cool vibes', and Ethos, for thirtysomething 'ambience' — the security guards have started frisking the highly-scrubbed clubbers.

Despite the whiff of pre-packed hedonism and corporate tackiness, Leisure World is bustling. Indeed, it may well be the future.

Pleasure dome: Life inside the transatlantic shape of things to come.

Rank Leisure has invested £22 million in the complex, which opened six weeks ago on the outskirts of Hemel Hempstead: it is the latest in an explosion of edge-of-town 'leisure box' developments. Its gigantic neon sky-writing suggests that a piece of America has landed on the lawn of England.

'Everyone's talking about "leisure boxes" at the moment,' says Stephen Yarnold, of property consultants Harvey Spack Field, which has been involved in a clutch of boxes (they are also known as 'multi-activity parks' or 'leisure parks').

'People find town centres too threatening in the evenings, and they will travel to find everything under one roof,' adds Mr Yarnold.

THI, a specialist leisure developer, has opened four 'boxes' in Britain and has another 13 under construction, at £25m apiece. According to Carl Lewis, THI's managing director, they will each draw up to two million people a year, spending at least £7 a night per person.

The heart of each 'leisure box' is the multiplex cinema, but when customers find so many other leisure pursuits under one roof, they tend to linger after credits, visiting a nightclub or taking in some bowling, bingo or skating.

After a few visits, they start turning up whether there is a film they want to see or not. And in the latest sign of the relentless Americanisation of British popular culture, the clients are also eating out, contrary to the Great British tradition. Last year 4 per cent of Britons ate out at least once a week, compared with 69 per cent of Americans, but we are catching up fast.

Mr Lewis, who is building leisure boxes in Sheffield, Dagenham, Leeds, Luton, Bristol and Chingford, acknowledged the transatlantic debt: 'We are following the Americans; people want to drive safely somewhere for a meal with the family, and to enjoy themselves for the rest of the evening.'

One hundred yards from Leisure World's garish blue neon sign is the garish *red* neon sign of an out-of-town Tesco store. This is no coincidence. British leisure is joining British retailing in an exodus from the town centre to its edges. Small wonder the towns themselves are becoming disorientating.

'Hemel itself is a lot quieter since this place opened,' said Bill Lewis, a local taxi-driver. 'I know one pub in town which is down four grand a week.'

The cloud hanging over the town centre opens up to reveal the taxi-driver's silver lining: 'It's unbelievable for business. I'm back and forth here all the time; on the weekend, half of them get completely wrecked and have *got* to call a cab.'

The boom in out-of-town development has fuelled fears that ghost towns are being created and green areas are being unnecessarily concreted over.

Such concerns prompted a government policy change last year, with a Department of Environment policy guidance note on leisure and tourism recommending that facilities such as cinemas be concentrated in town centres.

Alarmed at such a U-turn, property developers believe the Government may be failing to grasp that, in the Nineties, people want to feel safe in the evenings — which is not the case in town centres — and that, American-style, they are willing to travel up to 50 miles for a comprehensive evening's entertainment.

David Vaughan, managing director of Rank Leisure, says parking spaces offer the key to locating 'leisure boxes'. He needs 12 acres for every development, but he cannot handle land prices in town centres.

'Leisure boxes', he says, are the new wave of the Nineties: 'We'll build them wherever we can get the right sites.'

> 'We'll build them wherever we can get the right sites'

FIGURE 5.1 *Pre-packed fun in the pleasure dome*
SOURCE: *The Observer* 8 October 1995

REVIEW OF THE UNIT

TASK 6

STAFFING THE LEISURE BOX

Carefully read Figure 5.1, a newspaper article describing the introduction of multi-entertainment leisure boxes to the UK. For this task you are asked to take the role of the Human Resources Director of a company planning to site a leisure box in your local area.

- Suggest an appropriate organisational structure for the personnel of the new facility, bearing in mind each of the different attractions within the complex will be run by a specialist manager. Give reasons for your choice of structure and rejection of other models. Illustrate your proposal with an organisational chart
- Your company is keen that the new leisure box will stage special events such as Fun Days or themed entertainments, as well as its regular attractions. Include provision for the formation of ad hoc teams within your suggested organisational structure. Describe a sample ad hoc team that would be created for a special event of your choice and illustrate its formation on a copy of your chart
- The majority of staff for the leisure box will be recruited locally. Draw up job descriptions and person specifications for three positions in any one attraction within the complex; one at operative level, one at supervisory level and a third at managerial level. What choice of media would you use to advertise each of the three posts?
- You have the job of compiling several chapters of the staff handbook for the new facility. Briefly list the major points you should include for the following chapters:
  - Relevant legislation – regarding health, safety and employment
  - Workplace standards and conditions
  - Standards of staff performance and behaviour
  - Relevant occupational standards

CHECKLIST OF PORTFOLIO EVIDENCE

- ☑ Written report outlining proposals for structure of new facility, including organisational charts.
- ☑ Sample job description and person specifications.
- ☑ Outline of points to be included in staff handbook chapters.

Useful Addresses

ABTA
55–57 Newman Street
London
W1P 4AH

Advisory Conciliation and Arbitration Service (ACAS)
27 Wilton Street
London
SW1X 7AS

Commission for Racial Equality (CRE)
Elliot House
10–12 Allington Street
London
SW1E 5EH

Commission of the European Communities
Jean Monnet House
8 Storey's Gate
London
SW1P 3AT

Data Protection Registrar
Wycliffe House
Water Lane
Wilmslow
Cheshire
SK9 5AF

Department for Education and Employment
Sanctuary Building
Great Smith Street
London
SW1P 3BT

Equal Opportunities Commission (EOC)
Overseas House
Quay Street
Manchester
M3 3HN

Health and Safety Executive Information Centre
Broad Lane
Sheffield
S3 7HQ

Institute of Personnel Management
IPM House
Camp House
Wimbledon
London
SW19 4UX

NCVQ
222 Euston Road
London
NW1 2BZ

SCOTVEC
Hanover House
24 Douglas Street
Glasgow
G2 7NQ

Trades Union Congress (TUC)
Congress House
23–28 Great Russell Street
London
WC1B 3LS

Glossary

Ad hoc teams (or project teams): groupings of staff created for a specific short-term purpose.

Appraisal: an evaluation of the performance of an employee as a mechanism to recognise and improve good practice.

Competency: the ability to usually carry out a task correctly.

Compulsory Competitive Tendering (CTT): the procedure whereby organisations may tender bids for contracts to manage local government services.

Councillors: elected to serve on local government councils.

Directors: company officials elected by shareholders to manage the business.

Dismissal: the ending of an employee's employment with an organisation. This should follow fair procedures, for example, several warnings should be given before dismissal.

Executive director: involved in the running of a business on a full time basis.

Human resource management (HRM): the management of the workforce within an organisation. Specialist human resources or personnel staff are particularly concerned with HRM.

Human resources: the workforce of any organisation, both full time, part time and voluntary.

Induction: a period of training and acclimatisation to introduce new employees to their job.

Industrial tribunal: an informal court where legal disputes concerning unfair dismissal or discrimination can be heard.

Job description: a statement of the tasks, duties and accountability of a specific job.

Lines of authority: channels of communication, control and accountability within an organisation.

Manager: usually responsible for the staff and successful operation of a department or function within an organisation.

Managing director: the director responsible for day-to-day running of a company.

Matrix structure: a flexible type of organisational structure allowing the creation of project teams.

Non-executive director: part-time directors who attend board meetings, often appointed for specialist knowledge or contacts.

Operative: employees performing day-to-day tasks within an organisation (may also be termed assistants).

Organisational structure: how staff are grouped within an organisation to facilitate communication and control.

Organised teams: staff groupings established on a permanent or long-term basis to perform a specific function.

Person specification: a statement of the qualities and aptitudes of an ideal candidate for a job.

Private sector: organisations owned by private individuals.

Public sector: local or central government owned or controlled organisations.

Redundancy: staff becoming unemployed as their function or skills are surplus to requirements.

Shareholders: owners or part-owners of a business.

Span of control: the number of subordinate staff a manager or supervisor is responsible for.

Supervisors: 'first line managers' responsible to a manager for the performance of a group of employees.

Index

ABTA 52
ACAS 45, 52
ad hoc teams 15, 55
applications 25, 27, 36–7, 39, 40–2
appraisal 46

British Airways vi

centralised (structure) 2
Compulsory Competitive Tendering (CCT) 6
contract of employment 33, 34–5
councillors 6
CVs 27, 36–8, 40–1

Data Protection Act 46
decentralised (structure) 3–4
desktop publishing 51
directors 6
dispersion diagram 20–1, 22–3
divisional (structure) 3

equal opportunities 33–4
executive director 6

flat (structure) 2
functional (structure) 3

Guildford Spectrum Leisure Complex 3, 4, 16

health and safety legislation 45–6
hierarchical (structure) 3
Horsham Museum 2–3

induction 25, 43–4
interquartile range 20, 22
interviews 25, 27, 39, 40–2, 44

job description 25, 49, 55

lines of authority 17

management style 5–6, 19
   authoritative 5
   consultative 5
   democratic 6
   passive/laissez faire 6
managing director 6
matrix structure 15, 16

National Targets for Education and Training 50
non-executive director 6
NVQs 41, 47, 50, 52

organisational structure 1, 2–6, 10–11, 15–16, 55
   centralised 2
   decentralised 3–4
   divisional 3
   flat 2
   functional 3
   hierarchical 3
organised teams 15

Panorama Holiday Group Ltd 7–13, 15, 17–19, 25–33, 52
Pearson PLC 3, 5
person specification 25, 55
personnel records 46
project teams 15

recruitment 24–42

Scalar principle 6
shareholders 6
span of control 3
SVQs 47

teams 14–23
   ad hoc 15
   organised 15
   project 15

workplace legislation 44–6